WITCHES:
A PSYCHOANALYTIC EXPLORATION
OF THE KILLING OF WOMEN

WITCHES:
A PSYCHOANALYTIC EXPLORATION
OF THE KILLING OF WOMEN

EVELYN HEINEMANN

Translated by Donald Kiraly

'an association in which the free development of each
is the condition of the free development of all'

FREE ASSOCIATION BOOKS / LONDON / NEW YORK

First published in 2000 by
FREE ASSOCIATION BOOKS
57 Warren Street, London W1P 5PA

Copyright © Evelyn Heinemann 2000
Translation © Donald Kiraly 2000

The right of Evelyn Heinemann to be identified as the author
of this work has been asserted by her in accordance
with the Copyright, Designs and Patents Act 1988.

A CIP catalogue record for this book is available from
the British Library.

ISBN 1 85343 477 9 hbk; 1 85343 478 7 pbk

Designed and produced for Free Association Books Ltd by
Chase Production Services, Chadlington, OX7 3LN
Printed in the European Union by TJ International, Padstow

Contents

	Preface	vii
	Introduction	1
1	**The Persecution of Witches**	5
	Witchcraft Trials and the Persecution of Witches	5
	Did Women's Power Underlie the fear of Witches?	18
	The Notion of Witches	24
2	**How Women Became Witches**	30
	Accusations of Witchcraft	30
	The Psychoanalysis of Witchcraft Accusations	34
	The Accused Women	38
3	**The Fear of Witches**	43
	God and the Devil, the Virgin Mary and the Witch	43
	The Psychogenesis of the Notion of Witches and the Devil	45
	Childhood in the Early Modern Age	51
4	**The Early Modern Age**	57
	Society	57
	The Drives and the Ego	61
5	**The Psychic Conflict**	68
	The Reformer	68
	The Possessed	71
	The Changeling	78
	Child Witnesses	81
	The Living Saints	86
6	**Psychoanalysis and History**	91
	Freud	91
	Psychoanalysis and Historians	106
	Psychoanalysis and Culture	115

7	**The Study in the Light of Psychoanalytic Theory**	124
	Witches, Saints and the Superego	124
	Possessed Women and Hysteria	136
	Witches and Living Saints Today?	141
	Bibliography	144
	Index	154

Preface

In order to understand complex historical phenomena such as witch persecutions and psychic conflicts in the Early Modern Age, it is necessary to consider both historical and psychoanalytic findings, a combination regarded as problematic by experts in both fields. The application of psychoanalytic methods cannot be a substitute for the study of historical sources. Indeed, one depends on the historians' knowledge since sources are often completely inadequate which makes them difficult to comprehend. On the other hand, without psychoanalytic knowledge, it is not possible to understand the phenomenon of possession, the fear of witches, belief in the Devil and what all this meant to the people of the Early Modern Age.

Chapters 1–5 provide the historical foundations with respect to each phenomenon analysed in the book. Chapters 6 and 7 discuss the historical phenomena with regard to psychoanalytic theory.

Chapter 1 provides a historical survey of the time of the witch persecutions. With the help of source material, it discusses the proceedings of witch trials, witch ordeals, statements made by witnesses, witches' confessions and the kinds of torture applied. Popular notions of how witches performed their magic are also described.

Chapter 2 deals with the question of how ordinary women in the Early Modern Age became witches. The conflicts on which the witchcraft accusations were based are described and understood through psychic defence mechanisms. Historical sources on the situation of women in the Early Modern Age are also presented, proceeding on the assumption that the accused women were not witches, but victims of a process of projection.

Chapter 3 sets the stage for a deeper understanding of the notions of witches and the Devil. It describes this world of imagination with regard to increasing splitting processes. As psychoanalytic theories require knowledge of psychic development in childhood, historical research on childhood in the Early Modern Age is summarised.

The fear of witches and witch persecutions cannot be ascribed merely to conflicts in early childhood. For this reason, Chapter 4 deals with the development of society, with the increasing suppression of drives and the changes in the ego and the superego, all of which are reflected in the Reformation and the Counter-Reformation. A central conflict of that time seems to have been the extreme splitting mechanisms combined with new demands on people's superego structures.

In Chapter 5, psychic conflicts among people at large are described on the basis of individual groups of people affected by the witch persecutions in different ways. The changed superego structure is recognisable in Martin Luther's problems. The symptoms of possession stand for the conflicts of young women and have to be distinguished from accusations of witchcraft. Disabled children who were called changelings and who, starting in the Early Modern Age, were thought of as the products of sexual intercourse between a witch and the Devil, became victims of witch persecutions as well. The chapter continues with a description of the psychic situation of child witnesses who accused themselves of having had sexual intercourse with the Devil, but who also accused others of being witches. Finally, the living saints of the thirteenth to fifteenth centuries, who became a type of forerunner for the phenomena of possession and witchcraft, are described.

In Chapter 6, the methodological options for associating psychoanalysis and history are examined. Freud's approach and his explanations of possession, hysteria and the fear of witches are analysed and defined as historically problematic. After a summary of the discussion on psychoanalysis and history, a study of witch persecutions based on Freud is critically reviewed.

In Chapter 7, an attempt is made to show that the psychic conflicts of the living saints and the possessed, as well as the fear of witches, are the consequences of a defence mechanism developed in the process of adaptation to life in the Early Modern Age. The main focus is on the changes of oedipal processing, and of the superego. The distinction between the different kinds of conflicts in child witnesses as well as the distinction between possession and hysteria are of great interest from a psychoanalytic perspective. Are there common as well as different defence mechanisms? Is it possible to gain knowledge from historical phenomena which can be used in the contemporary theory of psychoanalysis?

The study concludes with reflections on fantasy and reality, on the risks and opportunities which the notion of witches provides as an image for psychic development in society at that time and today.

Introduction

" The crowd of spectators began to stir. Two open, horse-drawn carts started to make their way through the throng, while constables led the 'poor sinners' down the steps of the Town Hall. The executive justice and the deputy magistrate left the judicial enclosure and mounted their horses. Meanwhile, the executioner's assistants had fetched a brazier with glowing charcoal and placed it in front of the Town Hall, where it was cordoned off by bailiffs. The condemned prisoners were led into this open space. The executioner tested the pincers, large iron tongs, the ends of which had been plunged into the smoking brazier. Then he walked up to Anna Pappenheimer, seized her linen shift with both hands at the neck, and ripped it open with one powerful tug, pulling it down over the old woman's bony shoulders as far as her waist. The other prisoners were also stripped bare to the waist in similar fashion. Pale, eyes downcast or wide with terror, they stood there between their guards. The people in the square, of whom only those in the first few rows could see this part of the execution, craned their necks, surged toward the spot, and had to be forced back by mounted guards ...

" The executioner drew the first of the red-hot pincers from the brazier and ripped six gaping wounds in the arms and torso of Paulus Pappenheimer, who uttered fearful screams of agony. In a moment, the executioner had the next pair of tongs in his hand and was carrying out the same cruel punishment on Gumprecht. And so all the offenders were 'ripped,' one after another. Finally the executioner sliced off Anna Pappenheimer's breasts ...

" According to chroniclers' reports, the severed breasts were rubbed around Anna's mouth and around the mouths of her two sons. Then constables seized the maimed criminals and thrust them onto the two carts, which were standing ready ...

" In the meantime, a kind of procession had formed on the market-place in a space that had been cleared of spectators. At a signal given by the executioner's assistants, indicating that the poor sinners' carts were ready to set off, the procession got underway. It was headed by one of the Munich poor-law guardians carrying a large crucifix. Then came ducal and municipal constables, wearing side arms and leather belts to signify their authority ...

" Up on the gallows hill, the milling crowd was filled with a carnival spirit. Constables and grain stewards were hard put to it to hold back the curious from the six massive stakes and the 'griddle.' Even long after the tumbrils had reached the top of the hill, dense crowds of spectators were still streaming out from Munich; so the executive justice delayed the start of the execution ...

" A shout of 'Silence! Silence!' rang out over the place of execution. The tumult of the crowd, the shouting, singing, laughing, murmuring died down, and the attention of everyone present was focused on the summit of the gallows hill, which could be seen clearly from all sides. Christoph Neuchinger moved away from the group of horsemen waiting to the right of the stakes and guided his horse to the center of the hill. 'I order the executioner to carry out his duty,' he called in a voice that reached the very outskirts of the crowd, 'and I warrant him peace and safe conduct, whatever may befall him!' ...

" The executioner and one of his assistants dragged Paulus Pappenheimer to the wooden grating, laid him on it, and bound his arms and legs. Then the executioner took up the wheel with his brawny arms and let it fall, first on the right arm, and then on the left arm of the condemned man. The bones snapped with a loud crack, and the victim groaned aloud ...

" The other criminals suffered the same treatment. Only Anna was spared the wheel. For reasons that lie buried deep in the mystic symbolism of penal practices, women could not be broken on the wheel ...

" In the case of Paulus Pappenheimer ... something even more appalling: impalement. This was one of the most revolting punishments ever devised by the human imagination and even in those days was hardly ever used ... This is done by inserting a sharply pointed stake into his posterior, which then is forced through his body, emerging through the head, sometimes through the throat. This stake is then inverted and planted in the ground, so that the wretched victims live on in agony for some days before expiring ... It is said that nowadays not so much trouble is taken with impalement as was once the case, but such criminals simply have a short spit thrust into their anus and are left to crawl thus upon the earth until they die ... Paulus Pappenheimer was forced to suffer it

... The victim's screams must have sent shivers down the spines of the spectators who crowded around on the summit of the gallows hill.

" Two brawny retainers seized the victim as he writhed groaning on the ground and dragged him up the wooden planks that formed the ramp leading up to one of the central stakes. There they left him bound on top of the heap of brushwood. Then Anna was pulled up onto the pile alongside and tied to a wooden chair that had been secured among the bundles of faggots ... Pitch torches were lighted and thrust rapidly, one after the other, into the dry brushwood ...

" The strident, monotonous voices of those offering up prayers mingled with the crackling of the fire, the excited cries of the crowd, the screams and coughing of the agonized victims, which grew ever fainter: 'Lord Jesus, for Thee I live! Lord Jesus, for Thee I die! Lord Jesus, I am Thine, dead and alive!' Thus a priest led the prayers, and a choir of the faithful repeated the words ... Thick clouds of smoke darkened the blue and white of the summer sky. One by one the piles of burning brushwood collapsed, and finally the glowing stakes in the center of each pile also crumbled. By that time the fire had burned down so far that the executioner could risk approaching it. He took up his position on the highest point of the hill and called out loudly across the grisly scene: 'Worshipful justice, have I properly executed sentence?' Whereupon Neuchinger, still mounted, replied: 'Insofar as you have done execution as the law and the sentence demand, I declare that it remain so!'

" With this act, the execution was completed. The crowd slowly dispersed and straggled back to Munich along the Pasing highway. Up on the hill, with its smoking embers, only the knacker remained with one or two of the excutioner's assistants, who were detailed to clear up the site. Soon new fires would be built here. (Kunze 1987, pp. 406–14)

It must have been like this or at least similar for several thousand cases in which it was predominantly women who lost their lives at the stake. Although the figures of the different sources vary considerably, the estimated number of people burnt as sorcerers and witches in Europe between 1480 and 1780 is 100,000 (Behringer 1987b, p. 165). How could this have happened?

If we try and answer this question from the point of view of psychoanalysis, we find that we are less concerned with the political, economic and juridical conditions affecting the witch persecutions, since much has been publicised on this topic over the last few years, but more with the psychological state of mind of the people living at that time. Two questions are especially critical: who were the women burnt as witches, and what was going on in people's minds; what unconscious motives made them expose a woman to such a cruel destiny as the stake by calling her a witch?

The description of the witch executions makes one thing blatantly clear: while, without doubt, the state and the Church had a political interest in the witch trials, such as the disciplining of annoying opponents, such large-scale witch hunts could not have occurred without the approval of the population.

Witch executions met with great enthusiasm among the population. They often took place as veritable public festivals. Even if we consider the authorities' economic and political interests or their misogyny as possible motives for the witch trials, this aspect does not answer the question as to why women in particular were accused of being witches and why, at that time of all times, the fear of witches was so intense.

1   The Persecution of Witches

Witchcraft Trials and the Persecution of Witches

Witch persecutions in Europe were most prevalent between 1550 and 1650, historically the age of the Renaissance. The period from 1550 until 1800 is considered to be the beginning of modern times. The leading minds during the Renaissance, from about 1500 to 1620, came from the south, from Spain and Italy. 1620 to 1660 was the period of revolution, radical social change and the emergence of capitalism. From 1660 until 1800, the Age of Enlightenment, the direction of intellectual development shifted north, to England, Holland and France. The period before the outbreak of the persecution of witches, about 1000–1500, is generally classified covering the High and the Late Middle Ages. The sixteenth and seventeenth century persecution of witches did not stem from the 'Dark Ages', but from the beginning of modern times (Trevor-Roper 1970). The following chronological summary (Brackert 1977b, pp. 315–23) outlines the major stages of witch persecution.

500–900	The penitential books amply verify the common belief in fortune-tellers, destructive witchery and storm-raising. The Church considers it sinful, and combats this age-old belief.
643	King Rothar forbids the execution of women who have allegedly eaten people alive (Lea 1913, vol. 3, p. 464).
906	The *Canon episcopi* is issued. It remains a binding clerical statute for centuries. According to the *Canon episcopi*, witcheries are delusions and illusions caused by the Devil. Anyone who believes in such delusions is considered a Devil's child.
c. 1000	The Church attacks the Cathars in France. This group believes that the Devil rather than God has created the physical world, and that he keeps the soul bound to the body. Thus it is the soul's task to

	gain independence from this world in the fight against sensuousness.
c. 1150	Burning heretics to death becomes the common punishment in northern France and Germany.
c. 1200	The notion of witches is still widely spread among the people and clergy. However, there is still no collective notion of witchery.
1209	Pope Innocent III starts a crusade against the Albigenses, a heretical sect in southern France.
1227	In addition to the Episcopal courts, which had originally had ecclesiastical jurisdiction in cases involving heresy, Pope Gregory IX establishes the Inquisitional Courts. The responsibility of these courts is the persecution, conviction and execution of heretics. Compared to the traditional trial of indictment, in the inquisition trial the accused is almost completely stripped of his rights, which is justified by the gravity of the crime.
c. 1230	The newly established Inquisition already deals with the notion that during its gatherings, heretics would blaspheme against Christian sacraments, worship the Devil, dance and indulge in ritual orgies. Since the beginning of this century, these notions were also attributed to the puritanical Waldenses.
1252	Pope Innocent IV explicitly authorises the use of torture as a legitimate means in inquisitional trials, as does Pope Clement IV in 1265.
c. 1330	Some witch persecutors project the concept of the vassalic contract on the relationship between man and the Devil. According to them, such a contract would imply mutual obligations: the man who makes a pact with the Devil becomes his vassal, swears an oath of fealty and becomes entitled to the help of demons. The tradition of the feudal kiss probably provided the idea of the *osculum infame*,

the kiss of shame, which heretics were supposed to give the Devil, who was present in the shape of man or animal, on his behind.

c. 1350 — A clear mixing of many elements of the notion of witches with that of heretics can be observed. The transition to the fifteenth-century notion of witches now begins. Those convicted committed their disgraceful deeds due to their pact with the Devil. They were said to have had an illicit sexual relationship with the Devil and to have eaten children. At that time, women were not yet the main target of the Inquisition.

1398 — An expert opinion of the faculty of theology in Paris declares *maleficia* a fact; any relationship between man and the Devil is regarded as a rejection of God and is therefore heresy.

1400–1500 — There are 38 trials against witches and sorcerers in England, 95 in France and 80 in Germany. Many theological and canonical works argue against the *Canon episcopi* and thereby set the stage for a new era in the notion of what constitutes witchcraft.

1474 — Heinrich Institoris and Jacob Sprenger, who would later write *The Witch Hammer*, try to investigate mass persecution of witches in Upper Germany, that is, the Alpine region. However, they meet with fierce resistance.

1484 — Pope Innocent VIII issues his bull, appointing Institoris and Sprenger as Inquisitors in Germany and lists the essential *maleficia* of witches and sorcerers. It is also the first document of witch literature that was spread among the people in the wake of the invention of letterpress printing.

1487 — Institoris and Sprenger publish the *Malleus maleficarum, The Witch Hammer*, and cause the persecution now to concentrate on witches – that is, on women. To the present day, this work is regarded as the seminal encyclopaedia of witch hunting.

1500–1700	Intensive extermination of witches. The countless trials and executions in all parts of Europe cannot be portrayed here.
1563	Weyer publishes his famous book *De praestigiis Daemonum et incantationibus ac veneficiis*. Weyer was one of the first to dispute the theses of *The Witch Hammer*. While this Dutch doctor, like most of his successors, believed in the existence of the Devil, he also believed that the defendants in the witch trials were innocent. Weyer said that the witcheries were in fact pathological illusions and suggestions by the Devil. He considered confessions given under torture to be completely meaningless. The early end of witch trials in the Netherlands was due to his influence.
1631	Friedrich von Spee publishes the *Cautio criminalis*. He sharply criticises the proceedings of the witch trials. 'The nature of the trial was such that no innocent person would be spared', he writes.
1610	Last execution of witches in the Netherlands.
1684	Last execution of witches in England.
1736	England abrogates the penal law against witches.
1745	Last execution of witches in France.
1775	Last execution of witches in Germany.
1782	Last execution of witches in Switzerland.

The chronology of witch persecutions clearly shows two of its main preconditions. On the one hand, witch trials developed directly from inquisitional trials. Inquisitional principles of procedure were applied creating an important precondition for expanding the persecution of witches. On the other hand, the publication of the *Malleus maleficarum* – which spread rapidly due to the invention of the letterpress – was an important basis for the trials concentrating mostly on women. Both preconditions help explain the expanded trials and therefore the external conditions of the persecution. I will refer to the psychological causes later.

The *Malleus maleficarum*, written by Sprenger and Institoris, outlined a complete, theoretical line of reasoning explaining the existence of witches at the beginning of the sixteenth century. By emphasising black magic, they created the necessary conditions for the replacement of inquisitional trials with witch trials. To ascertain the principles of procedure of inquisitional trials, that is, secret written trials and torture as a form of evidence, and to keep the trials in secular courts at the same time, witchcraft was declared a *crimen exceptum*, an exceptional crime.

The fact that witchcraft was declared an exceptional crime left little chance for the accused to elude punishment. Witchcraft was put on the same level as the other exceptional crimes: treason, conspiracy, forgery and robbery with murder. Since all these crimes seriously endangered or harmed the community, people felt the usual laws were not strict enough. They wanted the state to use extreme measures to punish people for such crimes. The theory of exceptional crime led to radical changes regarding the indications of guilt, the length and intensity of torture, testimonies and denunciation. Compared with the usual practice of law, torture was used with a completely different intention. As part of the normal criminal proceedings in the Middle Ages, torture had formerly provided the possibility for a defendant who did not have any witnesses testifying in his favour to clear himself of suspicion by surviving the torture. In the witch trials, torture became a means to force a suspect to confess. The judge was even allowed to carry out torture more severely on the following day to achieve a confession at the second attempt. In order to begin torture, there had to be circumstantial evidence against the defendant. Thus the circumstantial evidence was increasingly seen as final proof of guilt since torture allowed no proof of innocence. Of all the different types of evidence, the confession carried the most weight, and a conviction based merely on testimonies or circumstantial evidence of guilt was not approved of by the secular rulers. On condition that guilt had been proven almost completely through circumstantial evidence, the judges ordered more and more torture with a clear conscience. Thus circumstantial evidence became the crucial part of the witch trial (Hammes 1977, pp. 92–9). But what was considered circumstantial evidence? Soldan and Heppe provide the answer:

" Everything! A bad reputation often based on a testimony made by a woman arrested by the inquisition, given out of hatred and under torture years before and often not even confirmed by witnesses; being named as an accomplice, being a descendant of a woman executed for witchcraft, being homeless, having led a wild and restless life, having gained considerable knowledge rather quickly, having uttered a threat followed by a sudden damage happening to the person threatened, being present in the fields shortly before a hail shower – all this appears to be something rather simple, but opposing things were taken as signs as well, in a way that those who wanted to avoid Scylla inevitably ended up in Charybdis. A successful treatment was often no less fatal than being accused of having caused harm. The accused woman had given laurel berries to her sick daughter-in-law whereupon she recovered. The prosecutor then drew the conclusion that the woman herself had caused that disease through witchcraft ... Those who attended church services only sporadically were under suspicion but those who attended church services regularly were suspected as well, for their behaviour showed the intention to divert suspicion from themselves. If somebody appeared to be frightened or scared when arrested, it was interpreted as a sign of a bad conscience. If he appeared calm and brave, the devil had made him headstrong and stubborn. But the most fatal evidence was the testimony of a witch who, upon being asked for the name of accomplices under torture, named any person in order to be relieved from her agony, and that person was then arrested immediately' (Soldan and Heppe 1912, p. 325).

Not all of the aforementioned circumstantial evidence was of equal value. A denunciation which was brought forth by someone sentenced to death and not withdrawn at the last minute gained the greatest importance for the judges, as well as with regard to the spreading of trials. Even a witch was considered honest when facing death. The witch was offered a considerable incentive if she held to her denunciation: namely the promise that in this case she would not be burned alive but killed in as painless a way as possible before being burned. Some of the condemned were first decapitated or strangled by the executioner when already tied to the stake. Often, the accused were promised that they would escape torture if they named enough accomplices to satisfy the court, as the witch hunters wanted the number of denunciations to be as high as possible. Needless to say, this promise was rarely kept. The accusation made by a witch was considered normal testimony. The witch trials were different from ordinary trials in this respect as well. As witchcraft was a crime difficult to prove, the presumption of the guilt of a defendant was considered to be sufficient evidence. It was only at the beginning of the witch trials that the defendant was first given the right of testimony so that the denunciation made under torture was fully accepted. The concept of the witches' sabbath then led to a torrent of trials. Since every witch was supposed to take part in the sabbath, which meant that she went to see many other witches, the court tried to find her accomplices with the help of confessions. Out of despair and excruciating pain, the convicted witches named alleged participants in the sabbath. Hated or envied persons were of course preferred. In the seventeenth century, at the climax of the persecutions, no one was safe any more (Hammes 1977, p. 102–7). The rules concerning the death penalty established by the court of Charles V, for example, permitted witnesses to testify only if they were deemed satisfactory and were of good repute. The *Malleus maleficarum*, in contrast, allowed anyone to be a witness. Little was done to ensure the integrity of the witnesses. This was also part of the theory of exceptional crime. Every means was accepted if it made it easier for the judges to prove the guilt of the accused. The following example shows to what excesses the freedom of the court could lead:

> Several witches had been accused of having exhumed a recently buried child in order to use it as an ingredient for their magical ointment. After being tortured repeatedly, every single woman confessed her guilt. The husband of one of the accused women insisted on having the child's tomb opened in the presence of a priest and other witnesses; this was at least a small success for the new method. The child was found unscathed in the tomb. Then, however, the free assessment of the evidence proved to be nevertheless damaging for the accused women. They were sentenced to death at the stake on the grounds that the child in the tomb was nothing but an artifice created by the demons. (Hammes 1977, p. 105)

In a great number of German trials, children appeared as informers or witnesses and were fully accepted by the court. Kuczynski mentions one case in which a grandmother was executed because of the testimony of her seven-year-old grandchild.

> In 1629 a seven-year-old girl called Gertrud Biel from Ketzerbach stood trial in Marburg. How much this delusion had poisoned the souls of the people can be seen in the confession of the little girl. The child aroused suspicion when, during a game with schoolmates she mentioned that she could do magic and had learnt it from her grandmother. 'Look, this is how you make weather,' she said and lifted her skirts. Her teacher promised the child a gold piece to get more out of her. She replied that she could not say

anything because otherwise her grandmother, called 'the Prussian,' would hit her hard. She admitted only that pushing a knife into a wall would conjure milk from the wall and that at home she milked the cows until they bled. Landgrave Georg noted this incident with the utmost regret, since the vice was already present in children. Since the girl was still very young, one could not accept what she said as evidence; the grandmother, however, who also was taken into custody, had to face the consequences. (Kuczynski 1980, p. 134)

Probably the best known trial involving child witnesses took place in the Swedish town of Mora in 1669. Based on the testimony of four-year old children, 72 women and 15 youths were sentenced to death (Hammes 1977, p. 109–11; Baschwitz 1990, p. 318). I will discuss the problem of child witnesses in more detail in Chapter 5.

As a witch trial did not focus on a crime which had actually been committed, but merely on assumptions about a person's attitude, the court needed other means, in addition to circumstantial evidence, to create the preconditions for inflicting torture. This was the purpose of the witches' ordeals. At first, the witches' test was only supplementary, albeit significant, circumstantial evidence, but soon it was regarded as primary evidence.

There were all kinds of witches' ordeals. The water test was adopted from mediaeval trials, whereas the needle test and the weighing test were exclusively invented for witch trials. For the water test, the accused was thrown into water three times with her hands and feet tied together. The court, often in the presence of the whole village, watched carefully to see whether the accused would float or sink. If she floated, she was proved to be a witch; if she sank, she was innocent. It was assumed that witches weighed less than ordinary people because their body was inhabited by a 'light and airy spirit'. There is no need to point out that in the course of this procedure many died through drowning even though they were in fact innocent in the eyes of the court.

The weighing test, too, originated from the idea that witches and warlocks weighed less than ordinary people. If the body weight was not in proportion to the person's height and shape, the accused was guilty. The witches' ordeal that was applied most frequently and for the longest time was the needle test. The skin was examined for blemishes, warts, scars or liver spots which were considered to be witches' marks. Since it was commonly believed that these marks were insensitive to pain and would not bleed when pricked, this was all that had to be done to obtain evidence. Normally all women had these so-called witches' marks. However, in all witches' ordeals there were deceitful manipulations by executioners and torturers. The so-called tear test was rarely applied. The inability to shed tears under torture was regarded as strong evidence to prove someone guilty. In some cases, the 'cauldron snatch' or hot water test was applied. The accused had to snatch a ring from the bottom of a cauldron filled with boiling water without hurting herself. Another way of proving her innocence was to walk through fire in a shirt soaked with wax without any of it dripping from the shirt.

In earlier court procedures, a confession was decisive proof of the accused person's guilt, and was therefore enough to justify a conviction. The confession was considered *Regina probationum*, the 'queen of proof law'. Though in the witch trials it was the court that had to conclusively prove the guilt of the accused, the confession did not lose its original status. The lack of witnesses did not lead to an acquittal due to lack of evidence, but instead the court insisted that the accused confess. If he or she did not do so voluntarily, the accused was submitted to meticulous questioning, that is, torture. In witch trials, where proof of guilt could not be produced except through a confession, the main purpose of torture was almost exclusively to yield a confession and to force the tortured person to denounce other people. The guilt of the accused was considered proven merely by circumstantial evidence and only had to be complemented by a confession. Only an insignificantly small number of accused witches confessed without having been tortured (Hammes 1977, pp. 111–23).

The torture actually began outside the chamber of torments with the threat of applying it. After that, the prisoner was led inside the torture chamber; she was stripped naked, tied to a rack, and her hair was cut off. Torture was carried out in five rounds, during which careful attention had to be paid that the accused did not die. Soldan and Heppe (1912) describe the process of torture as follows:

" Usually the torture began with the thumbscrews; the accused was stripped and tied up and his thumbs were put into the screws. By slowly tightening the screws his thumbs were crushed.

" If this did not work, Spanish boots, or leg screws, were applied, pressing the calf and shin together, often until the bones splintered. To increase the agony, the screws were struck with a hammer now and then. So that he would not be disturbed by the wailing of the tortured, the executioner put a capistrum into the victim's mouth, making screaming impossible.

" The next degree of torture was pulling, expansion or elevation.

During this treatment, the accused's hands were tied behind their backs and then fastened to a rope. The rope was suspended to a hook in the ceiling from which the victim was dangled in the air in one moment ... and in the next fastened to an upright ladder whose rungs often had short sharp pieces of wood, the 'jugged hare.' He was slowly pulled into the air until his arms were twisted over his head, whereupon he was rapidly dropped several times, and then, 'gently' pulled up again. If still no confession was forthcoming, heavy weights were attached to the tortured person's feet to stretch them even more terribly and painfully. The victim hung for half an hour, or often a full hour or even longer like this, and from time to time the Spanish boots were put on him as well.

" A new torture method was introduced in 1660 in Zurich. Two boards with wooden nails were tied to the feet and knees, these were used to stretch witches six hours every day 'until cramps ran through all their veins.' It might happen that during this period that the court personnel would leave to refresh themselves with food and drink.

" Von Wächter reports that, according to a protocol taken down in Bamberg, 'that a man accused of sorcery was tortured three and a half hours with leg screws and thumbscrews, and in the end, because he did not confess, he was pulled eight feet from the ground with a rope, and a weight of 20 pounds was attached to his toe. If even this or similar torture did not work, torturers trickled burning sulfur or pitch onto the naked body of the victim, or held burning lights under his arms, the soles of his feet or elsewhere' ...

" In the principality of Münster, the executioner used to break the arms and dislocate the shoulders of the accused in this last stage of the torture. The victim's arms were firmly tied behind his head and his henchmen pulled the victim up, so that his feet were several spans above the ground. In the pauses the executioner fastened the thumbscrews and the Spanish boots to the hands and feet of the victim to increase the pain. From time to time it was repositioned and tightened.Over and above this, the henchmen beat him with canes or leather straps, which were weighed down at one end with lead or equipped with sharp hooks, until the executioner told them to stop, so that the tortured person would not die. (1912, vol. 1, pp. 348–50)

Only pregnant women and children below the age of 14 were supposed to be exempt from torture, but this was not always the case (Hammes 1977, p.133). Specific methods for torturing women are not discernible from the court records (Brackert 1977a, p. 174). Men and women alike were put to the rack, as described above.

Most of the witch persecutions were made possible only due to their legal status as a *crimen exceptum*, that is, because they were derived from the trials of the Inquisitions. In England, where torture was illegal, only 19 per cent of the suspected witches and warlocks were executed after trial. Political as well as economical reasons contributed further to the growth of the witchcraft trials and consequently to the persecution of witches.

It was in countries such as the Netherlands or England, where the middle class had early won the fight for a voice in government, that witchcraft trials first met popular resistance and were quickly ended. In countries such as Spain, in which the monarch's reign was consolidated by the beginning of the sixteenth century, only a small number of trials were held in the first place. Germany, because of its complex governmental structure and history, saw the most violent witchcraft trials over the longest period of time. The trials were also ended first in those parts of the country where the absolutist government was firmly established, such as in Prussia at the beginning of the eighteenth century. For the government, witch persecutions were used as a means of discipline; the people being subjected to arbitrary rule. Unlike in the Middle Ages, a right to resistance no longer existed; the only thing granted was a right to appeal to the ruler who could meet this appeal if he wished to. As an example of how witchcraft trials were used in local politics, Brackert mentions the trials that raged in the Westphalian city of Lemgo at the end of the seventeenth century (1977a, p. 183). The authorities used the witchcraft trials as their most effective weapon against their critics and employed them to systematically eradicate their rivals, powerful families in the city. The victims tried to resist their eradication by repeatedly appealing to their Count, but either these appeals were not answered or the victims were punished for insurgency in addition to witchcraft. By maintaining this attitude, the Count supported the rule of terror in the city.

The political motives behind at least some of the witchcraft trials also become clear in the trial of Joan of Arc. She stirred up the French people against the English occupation forces. The Inquisitional Court which sentenced her to death was controlled by the English sovereignty. Thus, a politically unwelcome enemy could easily be removed (Grigulevic 1976, p. 231).

Witch persecutions were used as a means of discipline not only by the state but also by the Churches in their struggle for power. Historically, witchcraft trials took place in the same period that religious denominations were fighting for consolidation. Both Catholics and Protestants tried with all their might to achieve consolidation by violently suppressing their opponent's views. Both denominations alike took action against witches, although no such generalisation can be made for the whole of Europe. The Catholic clergy and the sovereigns set to work in the southwestern part of the German Empire, in Lorraine, Savoy or in France as eagerly as witch hunters in the Calvinistic Vaudois, in the Protestant parts of the Jura Mountains, in Scotland or England. On the other hand, more restraint was exercised in the Catholic parts of Northern and Central Italy, Spain, Portugal and in the Protestant parts of southwestern Germany, the Saar region and Alsace (Labovie 1991, p. 34).

With the help of geographical references, Trevor-Roper (1979, p. 188) shows that any significant outbreak of witch persecution occurred in regions where Protestant and Catholic areas adjoined one another and where religious disputes were no longer carried out on an intellectual level.

" The flare-up of the craze in the 60s marked the end of the period of the Protestant proclamation of faith. After that time, almost every outbreak of the witch-hunt lunacy that was limited to a particular place can be attributed to the aggression of one religion against the other. Religious wars led to the worst period of witch persecutions in French history. (Trevor-Roper 1979, p. 203)

A thesis often put forward in the literature on witch persecutions says that throughout the witchcraft trials, financial profit was an important factor regarding the motivation to carry out the trials (Soldan and Heppe 1912, vol. 1, pp. 438–47; Hammes 1977, pp. 243–57). Witchcraft trials were a profitable business for judges, executioners, lay judges, notaries, messengers and torturers. Up to 1532, the convicted peoples' possessions were usually confiscated, regardless of whether they had heirs or not. Most of the possessions went to lords of the land. Even after confiscation was banned in 1532, in practice nothing changed. There were many judges who, although they did not illegally confiscate goods, nevertheless acquired the possessions of the accused under pretence of covering the costs of the trials. As a result, the remaining spouses and orphans often found themselves in abject poverty (Hammes 1977, p. 248).

If condemned, the accused had to pay for any costs related to their trials, starting with food and drink when the court members met in a public house to discuss the action against a person under suspicion, and ending with the firewood needed for the stake. After the Thirty

Years' War, confiscation was re-established. Soldan and Heppe (1912, vol. 1, p. 473) remark ironically that the witchcraft trials became the new alchemy, turning human blood into gold.

Schormann (1981, pp. 80–9) makes the point that, at first sight, this thesis is in contrast to the clearly proven facts showing that most of the convicted persons belonged to the lower and poorer social classes. The victims' social and economic weakness has always been stressed. Looking at the detailed listings of the costs, it becomes clear that the persons directly involved in the trial, such as executioners, clergymen, messengers, court officials, town servants and many others, stood to gain significantly from the trials. This was not the case with the lords of the land. On the contrary, they were charged with the legal costs if the families concerned were insolvent. That is why in some places, additional taxes were raised in order to cover the legal charges. In a number of cases whole communities were obliged to provide a guarantee that the charges would be covered. Some orders were issued which tried to clamp down on the exorbitant expenses by specifying rates for the fees that could be charged.

A sort of burden sharing was created by re-establishing the confiscation of possessions. Thus, propertied victims were forced to contribute to the legal costs of the poorer ones. The coffers of the communities and the local rulers could no longer be expected to pay the high legal costs.

> If this claim is true, and if the confiscation of the possessions of the few really did only finance the court costs of the many, then we have another way of explaining the contradiction between the economic weakness of the majority of the victims on the one hand, and the simultaneous increase in affluence of the people carrying out the court case. This would allow others to carry the costs; not the authorities or the community, but instead the wealthier victims through the confiscation of their possessions. (Schormann 1981, p. 85)

The economic enrichment of a small part of the population may be regarded only as a marginal phenomenon accompanying witch persecution. In the Saar region, for example, about 43 per cent of the accused women belonged to the lower classes, that is, unpropertied people and beggars. Another 53.4 per cent belonged to the less propertied, and only 3.5 per cent were landowners, which approximately represented the general structure of the population (Labovie 1991, p. 176).

We see from this that the witchcraft trials and the persecution of witches were made possible by a series of motives in the political struggle for power, particularly on the part of legal bodies. Yet why were most of the persecuted persons women?

Did Women's Power Underlie the Fear of Witches?

Particularly at the beginning of the witchcraft trials, when they broke away from the trials for heresy, men were also often executed for being sorcerers (Dülmen 1982, p. 290). After this short period, women definitely represented the majority of victims of the witchcraft trials. A comparison of relevant tables on various parts of Europe shows that an average of 80 per cent of the victims were women, with maximum values of 95 per cent in certain Jura regions and 92 per cent in Essex and Namur, as well as minimum values of 58 per cent in the Vaud region and 64 per cent in Freiburg, Switzerland (Schormann 1981, p. 118). In Denmark, the percentage of women convicted was 90 per cent, while in Norway it was 80 per cent (Labovie 1991, p. 34).

The majority of the women accused in witchcraft trials were old, but we should bear in mind that in the Europe of the Early Modern Era, a 40-year-old person was already considered old (Schormann 1981, p. 119). About 50 per cent of the accused women in the Saarland were over 50. No less than 64 per cent of the imprisoned women were widowed, and of those, half had lived alone. Among the female population, the proportion of widowed women was very high during the period of the witch persecutions. At the beginning of the seventeenth century, the percentage was at 3.5–7.5 per cent, and this increased, from 1628 on, to 10–20 per cent in the years of war (Labovie 1991, p. 175).

According to Hammes (1977, p. 61), old women were the main victims of witch hunters who sought the path of least resistance and found it among old women. The majority of these women who lived alone and who were able to make a living only by begging, represented a marginal group which had no influence, but was numerous. The witchcraft trials started out as a war against old women who were weak, lonely and often unpopular (Baschwitz 1990, pp. 139–40).

In the further course of the witch persecutions, increasingly younger women were convicted, too. The envoy to the Reichstag of the landgrave Georg of Darmstadt wrote in 1582: 'Since we have all but eradicated the old ones, we will now go after the young.' (Hammes 1977, p. 61; Baschwitz 1990, p. 140). Towards the end of the trials in Würzburg in 1629, almost one victim in four was younger than 14 years of age (Hammes 1977, p. 61).

While the victims of witchcraft trials were usually women, the accusers in court were mainly men, which of course is also due to the particularly difficult position of women in court at that time. In Saarland, 80 per cent of the accusers in the witchcraft trials were men, three-quarters of the witnesses in trials against men were men, and two-thirds of the witnesses in trials against women were also men (Weber 1996, p. 63).

The explanation of why women became the major victims of witch persecutions can be seen in the Church's misogynistic attitude. The authors of the *Malleus maleficarum* (*The Witch Hammer*) considered the equation 'woman = witch' to be self-evident and easy to prove. They claimed that the Latin word *femina* ('woman') was formed from the Spanish word *fe* ('faith') and the Latin word *mina* ('less'), which made women those 'with less faith'. In conformity with the prevailing theological doctrine, the authors assumed that ever since the fall of Eve, women had been far less able to resist the Devil's seductive ways than men. However, according to the authors, one had to be careful when using the name Eve ('Eva' in German and most other European languages) in this context, since Eve's curse was annulled by the word Ave (Maria's blessing), that is, the word which is produced by reading 'Eva' backwards. As the *Malleus maleficarum* made sexual intercourse with the Devil along with the practice of evil witchcraft the central point of its theoretical framework, one thing was obvious: the Devil, being traditionally a male creature, mainly had to pursue women; and therefore his followers would also have to be mostly women (Sprenger and Institoris 1971, part 1, p. 44).

The fact that the witch theory increasingly assumed that witches belonged to the female sex must definitely be seen as being grounded in an ecclesiastical tradition which had always proclaimed the inferiority of women. It therefore goes without saying that even the ideology of the early opponents of the witch theory, such as Weyer, is based on that same misogynous tradition. Weyer, for instance, explains the greater female proneness to melancholy, and therefore women's proneness to being deceived by the Devil's pretences, on the grounds of their inferiority (Schormann 1981, pp. 116–22).

However, it is not sufficient to see witch persecutuions exclusively as a result of the Church's misogyny. In what way did the population support the authorities in the campaign against women?

A possible explanation seems to be the fear of women. This fear of witches was considered to be the fear of wise women who were experts in the use of herbs, able to control their own fertility and unwilling to submit to a patriarchy. Since the only explanations that had so far been taken into consideration were those comprehensible by logic and reason, while unconscious motives were disregarded, the fear of witches had to be linked to the actual characteristics of the convicted women. Thus, to cause fear, women had to avail themselves of very powerful skills.

One of those skills was supposed to be their knowledge of hallucinogenic drugs. These 'witches' were considered to be drug addicts and their flying experiences unusually realistic hallucinations. Duerr (1979, p. 15) has pointed out that most of the women convicted of witchcraft did not rub themselves with ointment. He writes that none of the minutes contained any reference suggesting that witch ointment had been found in the possession of the women in question. Without exception, those convicted had been quite ordinary farm workers and citizens. By asking leading questions, the judges imposed their ideas on the women who later confirmed them under torture. Although Duerr realises this contradiction to the historic situation, he nevertheless tries to hold on to his drug hypothesis. He is of the opinion that it was not the witches who rubbed ointment on their bodies, but night-flying women. These 'old hags with magic powers' used ointment made from plants and afterwards had the impression of flying through the woods. According to Duerr, this phenomenon was then attributed to witches.

For Becker et al. (1977, pp. 80–117), the witch was the woman physician of the Middle Ages, an obstacle to men's dominance and modern science. In their capacity as midwives and physicians, witches were responsible for the development of gynaecology. At the beginning of modern times, these healing women lost their autonomy. They were forced into the position of midwives controlled by physicians and the town council. Pushing women out of medical practice was considered primarily to be the result of a clash between two opposing medical principles: on the one hand, the women's healing skills, which were based on natural methods of treatment; and, on the other hand, the scientific and theoretical methods of the male medical profession. This clash resulted in a veritable smear campaign against women.

" One thing was sure: any kind of resistance put up during the Middle Ages by wise women skilled in medicine was broken down after the witch-hunt. Not only was the image of evil witches successfully spread by inquisitors; now people also applied this negative image to midwives and wise women, as it had been established in midwife books, and in the local council of midwifery. Medicine practised by women was dead; the 'scientific' medicine of males triumphed and thus prepared to conquer midwifery as well. (Becker et al. 1977, p. 116)

The women burned as witches were by no means the wise herbal experts and physicians of the people (Behringer 1987b, p. 151). It has not even been proved that midwives were really such a prime target of the persecutions. Labovie (1991, pp. 180–1) could not account for a single trial against a witch midwife in the Saarland. Nor is there any indication that Luther (Haustein 1990, p. 177) connected witches with midwives or wise women who used herbs.

It was only in people's notions of witches that midwives played a key role in the witch hierarchy. They were often regarded as witch princesses. It was obviously very easy for them to provide one of the indispensable ingredients of the magical ointments – a new-born baby who had not yet been baptised. Moreover, there was the possible threat of midwives promising the new-born babies' souls to the Devil without the parents knowing anything about it (Hammes 1977, pp. 61–6). However, this is not indicative of the true nature of witchcraft accusations.

" There is significant debate about why certain people were accused of witchcraft. It should be noted that the deliberate intention of extinguishing certain social, religious, or other existing groups was not related to this phenomenon. Midwives, for instance, were especially suspected of witchcraft by the misogynist authors of the *Malleus Maleficarum*. However, these were respected members of the society, employed and paid by the magistrates in the cities. The motive for staging witch trials was the fear of being exposed to a witch's spell. (Behringer 1987b, pp. 151–2)

Heinsohn, Knieper and Steiger (1979) also have a theory on the reasons for equating midwives with witches. They say that the overall persecution of witches had only been instigated to eradicate the midwives' knowledge of contraception. This perspective can, however, be regarded as completely unfounded. Indeed, the very idea of the authorities being responsible for a phenomenon of such dimensions is absurd in terms of mass psychology.

The real phenomenon of witch persecutions cannot be explained by reason. Neglecting unconscious motives, almost all explanations try to answer the question of what was so horrible about the women accused of being witches. Reasonable and conscious motives are sought, making the fear of witches appear plausible. The search for reasons behind the fear of witches targeted the so-called witches themselves and not those who accused them.

The theory of wise women with a profound knowledge of herbs, who might have existed, but who were, however, not identical with the women prosecuted as witches, lacks historical evidence, as does the idea that there might have been a clandestine cult of witches rooted deeply in the past. The theory of the witch cult was made popular by Murray (1931). Witches, in Murray's opinion, were followers of a religion that was older than Christianity and widely spread throughout society until the seventeenth century. The centre of that religion was the worshipping of a horned god, who was known as Dianus or Janus among the Romans. According to Murray, the witch cult is a dianic cult which was prevalent during the Middle Ages, while Christianity was merely a façade. It was not until the Reformation that Christians had enough power to take action against the witch cult. However, Murray cannot verify the cult's existence. She was an Egyptologist, archaeologist and ethnologist, but not experienced in historical methods. From Cohn's point of view (1975, pp. 109–25), this is the reason why she uses only 15 sources from Scottish witch trials for her research, a totally ahistorical approach, and one which infers the existence of a witch cult on the basis of confessions made by condemned women under torture.

According to Murray, the witch cult was often traced back to a fertility cult at the time of the Germanic tribes. Mayer (1936) draws connections between the witch cult and the ancient belief in the goddess of the earth, Mother Earth. Hecate, Demeter and Diana were personifications of Mother Earth. Diana and Holda were considered the leaders of witches. Thus it is typical for the witches' assemblies to coincide with the fertility feasts, the witches' gatherings in the month of May. According to Mayer, hobby-horses appear at all fertility dances. In many regions the witches' power was considered broken as soon as the hobby horses were lifted off the ground.

While Mayer merely points out certain obvious parallels between notions of witches and the old belief in Mother Earth, both of which belong to the domain of the imagination, Brenner and Morgenthal (1977, pp. 188–214) consider the fertility cult to be most central to witchcraft. The authors claim that witch cults really existed. According to Brenner and Morgenthal, women were the ones who preserved this magical fertility cult until the Middle Ages. In 'magical religion', elements of matriarchal societies continued on into the patriarchal society of the Middle Ages. The woman was a mediator between man and nature. In fertility rites she broke the patriarchal restriction of her sensuality. Witchcraft became the woman's rebellion against suppression. The witches' sabbath became the place of women's conspiracy against order and reason. Thus, the excesses of witchcraft, like cannibalism, are patriarchal perversions that have little to do with the actual fertility cult.

These explanations, however, do not have much in common with the historical witch. In the Early Modern Age, witches were considered a power that destroyed fertility, and this was the reason for their persecution. Here, too, the methodical approach of the authors is striking. In their work, they refer mainly to one source, Zacharias (1970), who verifies the existence of the supposed fertility cult, like Murray, with descriptions from a few court protocols of women who testified under torture.

Other theorists (see Honegger 1977, pp. 84–9) attempt to link the persecution of witches to fertility cults. According to Russell (1979), persecutions concentrated mainly on those areas where inquisition trials had previously taken place. Under the pressure of their persecutors, heretics fled into lonelier Alpine regions of Europe where magical fertility cults were still widespread. Later, the Inquisition judged these cult forms to be witchcraft, so that pagan interpretations were no longer important. Ginzburg's study of the agricultural cult of the Benandanti in Friuli, Upper Italy, has become the basic evidence for this thesis. In certain seasons, the Benandanti regularly fought battles against evil spirits. The purpose of these battles, which they fought without leaving their beds, was to save fields and crops from being damaged by evil forces. Influenced by the Inquisition, this old hallucinatory fertility cult was taken apart and modified enough to adopt the shape of classical witchcraft. From then on, the Benandanti participated in the sabbath, committed *maleficia*, created thunderstorms and destroyed the fields and crops which they had previously defended.

The research carried out on the Benandanti cannot prove at all that a magical fertility cult of witches existed. As Cohn (1975, pp. 123–5) emphasises, the Benandanti were lying in their beds, fighting only under hallucination. There were no gatherings which could be transformed into a witches' sabbath under the influence of the Inquisition. The notion of the witch cult must have been developed in the minds of inquisitors and persecutors beforehand and then applied to the Benandanti.

If the notions of witches in the sixteenth and seventeenth centuries, which are the only ones relevant in this context, developed from a fertility cult, its emergence must be sought in rural areas, because that is where fertility rites traditionally took place.

Using geographic data, Russell (1979, pp. 159–268) shows that this is obviously not the case. The notion of witches and their subsequent persecution began in the cities and in the most industrialised areas of Europe. In the Alps, the witch craze raged later, after the so-called witches had fled from industrialised areas to this region.

> Some areas of Europe were much more susceptible to witchcraft than others. Spain, though it had a strong tradition of high magic, had little witchcraft, which supports Trevor-Roper's view that the two phenomena are wholly unrelated. Portugal, southern Italy, Scandinavia and Ireland were also relatively untouched, as was England until the fourteenth century. Witchcraft was strongest in France, the Low Countries, the Rhineland, northern Italy, and the Alpine regions. With the exception of the Alpine regions, these areas were the richest, most populous, most highly industrialized, and most intellectually advanced in Europe. Witchcraft appeared in the Alps only after witches and heretics took refuge from persecution by fleeing to the safety of the mountains. The geographical facts thus strongly suggest that on this issue Lea, Hansen, Murray, Trevor-Roper, and even to some extent Runeberg and Ginzburg, all of whom have emphasized the agrarian or mountainous nature of witchcraft, are in error. This in turn gravely weakens the hypothesis that witchcraft was fundamentally a fertility cult that had its roots in agriculture or in hunting. (Russell 1972, p. 268)

The fear of witches did not emerge in rural areas but in those regions of Europe which were the most developed and intellectually progressive. There was neither a witch cult that developed from a fertility cult nor were the condemned women experts in biology or adept at processing narcotics. We have to banish the notion of witches in the sixteenth and seventeenth centuries to the imagination. Cohn (1975, p. 125) advises us not to underestimate the power of the human imagination which has created demons and creatures of the night all over the world.

The Notion of Witches

What were the characteristics which made witches in the Early Modern Age so dangerous in people's minds that it was considered necessary to have them identified and executed? The four crucial accusations were: harmful magic, fornication and making a pact with the Devil, and participation in the witches' sabbath.

The accusation of harmful magic, the *maleficium*, was focused on the skill of storm-raising. In 1585, Lerchheimer wrote, 'They made storms, rain at the wrong time, wind, thunder, hail, snow, hoar-frost, frost, caterpillars, beetles, and other vermin so that the grain harvest, the vines, the acorns and other crops on the fields shall rot' (Hammes 1977, p. 73).

One part of the skill of storm-raising was killing people or animals by means of lightning. Weather magic was particularly feared in rural areas where it increasingly became the central focus of the trials. Since storm-raising was originally attributed to God, *The Witch Hammer* also dealt with the question of what witches achieved only with the Devil's help when raising storms, what was exclusively to be attributed to the Devil and which of these works could only happen with God's permission (Sprenger and Institoris 1971, part 2, pp. 147–9).

One aspect of the *maleficia* was that witches were accused of causing impotence as well as infertility and illnesses in people and cattle. There are countless reports of instances of witches causing infertility and impotence. The removal of male genitals by a malevolent spell was mentioned quite frequently, although it was clear that their disappearance was no more than an illusion (Sprenger and Institoris 1971, part 2, pp. 118–22).

" First, it must in no way be believed that such members are really torn right away from the body, but that they are hidden by the Devil through some prestidigitatory art so that they can be neither seen nor felt. (Sprenger and Institoris 1971, part 2, p. 119)

Sprenger and Institoris tell of a youth from the city of Regensburg who, after deciding to leave his lover, thought he had lost his member. Taking the advice of an old woman, he lay in wait for the girl one night and choked her with a piece of cloth until she promised to heal him. She touched him between his thighs and when the youth looked down, his member had been given back to him (Sprenger and Institoris 1971, part 2, p. 119).

It was assumed that diseases were induced by witches; but only those that had been prophesised by a witch or that had occurred suddenly without explanation.

" It has sometimes been found that even these [diseases] have been caused by witchcraft. For in the diocese of Basel, in the district of Alsace and Lorraine, a certain honest labourer spoke roughly to a certain quarrelsome woman, and she angrily threatened him that she would soon avenge herself on him. He took little notice of her; but on the same night he felt a pustule grow upon his neck, and he rubbed it a little, and found his whole face and neck puffed up and swollen, and a horrible form of leprosy appeared all over his body. (Sprenger and Institoris 1971, part 2, p. 136)

Witches could also inflict illnesses on wild and domestic animals or even kill them by touching them or bewitching them with their 'evil eye'. Sometimes they put some kind of witches' spell under the threshold of the barn door or where the animals used to go to the drinking trough. Cows were the favourite object of sorcery: 'So also there is not even the smallest farm where women do not injure each other's cows by drying up their milk, and very often killing them' (Sprenger and Institoris 1971, part 2, p. 144). The stealing of milk was said to occur as follows:

> On the more holy nights according to the instructions of the Devil and for the greater offence to the Divine Majesty of God, a witch will sit down in a corner of her house with a pail between her legs, stick a knife or some instrument in the wall or a post, and make as if to milk it with her hands. Then she summons her familiar who always works with her in everything, and tells him that she wishes to milk a certain cow from a certain house, which is healthy and abounding in milk. And suddenly the Devil takes the milk from the udder of that cow, and brings it to where the witch is sitting, as if it were flowing from the knife. (Sprenger and Institoris 1971, part 2, p. 145)

The prerequisite for the practice of black magic, be it storm-raising or the causing of illnesses in humans or cattle, was a pact between the witch and the Devil. The concept of these pacts did not arise until the Early Modern Age. In exchange for the witches' salvation, the Devil provided them with supernatural powers which not only enabled but in fact obliged them to inflict damage on other people. The pact could only take effect if a visible sign existed for the concluded agreement. The most common sign for this pact with the Devil was the so-called *stigma diabolicum*, the witch's mark, with which the Devil branded his disciple when she attended the witches' sabbath for the first time. Irregularities of the skin, such as warts, scars and moles that were insensitive to pain and did not bleed when punctured with a sharp object, were all considered to be a witch's marks (Hammes 1977, pp. 77–81). Occasionally, a formal contract was concluded between the witch and the Devil and this had to be signed in the witch's blood (Leibbrand and Wettley 1967, p. 828).

It was commonly believed that in most cases, the pact with the Devil was sealed by sexual intercourse between the human being, a Devil incarnate, and the Devil. The Devil appeared to a female witch in his male form, as incubus (lying on top) and to a male witch as a female succubus (lying beneath). In these encounters, the Devil was incapable of procreation. The Devil incarnate simply acted as a sperm conveyor. In his female form, he received male sperm which he, in his male form, could then pass on to a woman. When tortured, the women confessed to having had intercourse with the Devil so that the world would become full of Devil incarnates. Children fathered by the Devil were called changelings. Deformed children and cripples who had supposedly been fathered by the Devil were exposed at fairs (see 'The Changeling' in Chapter 5).

Although the Devil was incapable of procreation, the number of his followers increased. Either the witches promised the souls of their children to demons, usually without the fathers' knowledge, or it was the witch midwives, who were identified as being particularly suspicious in the *Malleus maleficarum*, who did this in secret: 'As soon as the child is born, the midwife, if the mother herself is not a witch, carries it out of the room on the pretext of warming it, raises it up, and offers it to the Prince of Devils, that is Lucifer and to all the devils' (Sprenger and Institoris 1971, part 2, p. 141).

This claim of the *malleus maleficarum* had serious consequences. Kinship to a witch was seen as strong circumstantial evidence of witchery on the part of the suspect. The question as to whether a person's mother or father had been burned at the stake as a warlock or witch was the first question to be asked in interrogations. It was inferred from the parents' witchery that the children were also witches since in such cases they were usually thought to have been dedicated to the Devil. In this manner, entire families were eradicated.

From the sixteenth century on, attendance at the witches' sabbath was an essential part of witchery. Before flying to the place where the sabbath was held, the witch rubbed her body with a foul-smelling, watery liquid. Paracelcus enumerated the ingredients of such an ointment: mincemeat made from children, poppy, winter cherry and hemlock or lard of children, nightshade and blood of bats. Although the manner of preparation varied considerably, there were two ingredients in every magical ointment, namely herbs which could cause certain nervous reactions, and parts of a child's body. Nightshade, hemlock and henbane could cause mental derangements resulting from poisoning. After rubbing herself and her broomstick with ointment,, the witch uttered the incantation: 'Up and out to nowhere', and flew up the chimney to join the witches' sabbath. Occasionally, she also flew on a goat's back. In this respect, the witches' statements in the court records from different areas are almost identical (Hammes 1977, p. 64).

From a report on a witch trial held in Logrono, Spain, in 1610, I would like to quote excerpts of the most important and typical material regarding the witches' sabbath presented by the prosecution:

" After such a concession and promise [to renounce the Christian faith], the master, who has the task of teaching the candidate and who has convinced him to become a sorcerer, comes to his bedside or a place where he is sleeping or lying awake, about two or three hours before midnight on a witches' sabbath night. If the candidate is still asleep, he wakes him and anoints his hands, temples, chest, private parts and the soles of his feet with a dark green, smelly water and takes the candidates with him immediately. He carries them through the air, through doors and windows, which the devil opens for them or through another small gap or hole. In no time at all, they arrive at the place determined for their meetings, the place of the witches' sabbath. There, the sorcerer first presents the 'novice' to the devil, who is sitting on a throne which at times seems to be made of gold and at other times of black wood. The devil sits there with great dignity and majesty, and with an exceedingly sad face, ugly and bad-tempered ... His body and build are similar both to those of a human being and a goat, his hands and feet have fingers and toes like those of a human being, but they are all of the same length, tapering to a point, with sharp claws. Then the novice has to bend his knees in the presence of the devil, and he has to renounce the same things in the same manner which his mentor the witch had impressed upon him; the devil says the words with which he has to renounce his faith, and he (the novice) repeats them and renounces, first God, then the Virgin and Mother Mary ... Then he (the novice) accepts the devil as his God and Lord and worships him, pressing a kiss on his left hand, on his chest next to his heart and on his genitals. The devil turns over on his left side and lifts his tail (which is similar to that of a donkey), and lays bare those body parts which are extremely ugly and that tend to be particularly dirty and smelly. He is then kissed on those body parts beneath his tail. Afterwards, the devil stretches out his left hand and lowers it to the head and further down to the left shoulder or other body parts of the novice (depending on his mood), and marks the candidate by digging his claws into him. Thus he wounds him, making him bleed. Then the devil collects the blood in a cloth or in some kind of container. The wounds of the witch-novice causes him great pains which last longer than a month; and the mark and stigma remain for a lifetime.

" On the eves of certain annual holidays, they gather for the witches' sabbath in order to worship and celebrate the Devil, and they all confess to him and lament their sins. The women also make offerings such as loaves of bread, eggs, and other things which they hand to the devil's servants. The women then bend their kneels in reverence, kiss the devil's left hand and his chest close to his heart. Two sorcerers, who usually serve as the devil's train bearers lift his garments so that the women are able to kiss his genitals. The devil immediately turns to the left and his tail is lifted to reveal the parts that are very dirty and smelly. At that very moment when someone kisses the devil beneath his tail, the devil blows an awful smelling wind into her face. He nearly always does this when kissed in this way. All of the sorcerers then form a circle and receive communion from the devil. The hosts have the devil's likeness painted on them; these hosts have a disgusting odour and are hard to swallow. Afterwards, he also offers them a very bitter drink that turns their hearts cold.

" As soon as the devil has finished the mass, he copulates with both men and women in the manner of the Sodomites ... The queen [of the witches' sabbath] chooses the witches who are supposed to join the devil for this purpose and who are waiting at a distance ... As soon as the devil stops doing the aforementioned evil deeds and even more horrible things that we will leave out here, warlocks and witches mingle with each other, men with women, and even men with men, regardless of social status or the degree to which they are related to each other. (Zacharias 1970, pp. 56–62)

During court proceedings, inquisitors repeatedly asked the witches about these notions, and, under torture, the accused women answered the questions in the affirmative.

2 How Women Became Witches

Accusations of Witchcraft

The accused women neither belonged to a special social group or profession, nor were they in possession of any significant amount of magical knowledge. Thus the question remains open as to why ordinary women were suspected of acting in a manner consistent with the popular image of the witch. How did women become witches?

Witch accusations were the result of a conflict between the woman who had been accused of being a witch and her accusers. Labovie describes the women accused in the witchcraft trials in the German region of Saarland as rebellious, quarrelsome members of the community. For years they had often been connected with witnesses and accusers through social or personal family relations and dependencies.

> " The relationship between witnesses and accused seems to be characterised by ties as relatives, acquaintances, neighbours or lovers, as well as by work-related relationships and, above all, by personal conflicts of various kinds. In 59 per cent of cases, the accused and the witnesses came from the same community; in most of the remaining cases from an adjacent village or town. (Labovie 1991, pp. 189–90)

There were conflicts that led to aggressive encounters in the course of which the accused woman had usually been treated unfairly, and thus people feared her revenge. *Maleficium* was considered a typically female act of revenge. Therefore, the statements made by the witnesses concentrated on giving a plausible reason why the accused woman had taken revenge. *Maleficium* with the help of magic was feared as a female act of revenge and was an obvious choice for women, since taking legal action was much more difficult for them (Ahrendt-Schulte 1994, p. 177). As already mentioned, 80 per cent of the accusers in the witchcraft trials were men (Weber 1996, p. 63).

Thomas (1973; 1979) emphasises that the accused women had previously been victims of wrongdoing, so there was reason to fear their justified revenge. It could have been, for example, that they had muttered a few curses, but normally the women had not done anything that led to the harm they had been accused of. Witchcraft served as an explanation for otherwise inexplicable misfortunes like, for example, a mishap that occurred during an everyday chore, an illness, the loss of a domestic animal or the sudden death of a child. Especially when it came to illness, witchcraft was often used as an explanation (Thomas 1979, pp. 256–70).

The suspicion of witchcraft, however, only arose when a likely suspect had already been singled out. The accused woman was not usually a stranger, but lived in the neighbourhood or in the same village. In many cases she had a personal relationship with her alleged victim. After suffering misfortune, the victim remembered a threat or a similar remark and was now convinced that this person's aggression had caused the misfortune. This aggression, though, had to be justified: the witch had to have a good reason for cursing her victim.

" In cases where an appropriate reconstruction of the circumstances is possible, a closer examination shows that an accusation was usually only made if the plaintiff not only had the feeling that the witch held a grudge against him, but if her grudge was also justified. That is to say the witch was not considered to act out of a mere lust for revenge. She was reacting rather to a definite injustice. It was of no consequence whether the victim and the witch had quarrelled or not. Paradoxically, the emphasis lies upon the fact that it was the witch rather than the victim who was morally in the right. (Thomas 1979, p. 278)

Let us take a look at some examples that led to witchcraft accusations. In 1579, Richard Saunder's wife refused to give Margaret Stanton from Wimbish some yeast, whereupon her child fell seriously ill. Robert Cornell's wife refused to give Margaret some milk – shortly afterwards she developed a large growth. After John Hopwood had refused Margaret a leather belt, his gelding died (Thomas 1979, p. 280). A seventeenth-century house-owner gave the following description of such an encounter with an alleged witch:

" It was not long ago ... when an old man or an old woman came to my door and asked for alms which I refused and, may God forgive me, I felt an anger against her welling up inside of me ... and soon afterwards my child, my wife, I, my horse, my cow, my sheep, my pigs, my dog, my cat or something else behaved in so strange a way, that I could swear it was a witch, or how else could such things occur? (Thomas 1979, p. 279)

There was a variety of reasons which could provoke a witch to this kind of justified attack. Sometimes the victim had refused to repay a debt the witch had come to claim, for example, a woman might have bought eggs and not paid for them or a servant might have stolen his master's gloves.

The most common case, however, was that the victim had offended the norms of charity by shutting the door in the face of an old woman asking for food or drink, or trying to borrow some money or a household item. According to Thomas, the majority of the fully documented cases fit this simple pattern. The witch is sent away empty-handed and perhaps while walking away she mutters a curse and soon afterwards some misfortune occurs.

Hence witchcraft was a process which took place in the mind of the witch accuser and bore no relation to the actual behaviour of the women themselves. The women did not cause the harm they were accused of. The victim interpreted an incident caused by mere chance, such as a stroke of lightning, as harm caused by the witch because he expected her to harm him as a consequence of his own immoral behaviour. Fear of the witch's revenge, though, could also lead to self-inflicted harm, for example, in cases of illness and impotence. At times the fear grew so strong that the mere intention of carrying out an immoral action led to harm caused by the victims themselves.

The youth from Regensburg thought he had lost his member after *deciding* to leave his lover. Taking the advice of an old woman, he lay in wait for the girl one night and choked her with a piece of cloth until she promised to heal him. She touched him between his thighs and when the youth looked down, his member had been given back to him (Sprenger and Institoris 1971, part 2, p. 119) It was thus his own guilty conscience which showed in which direction to look for the cause of his misfortune.

Barbell Lauer, like the rest of her family, came from Merchingen (Germany), which had about 100–120 inhabitants in 1600. Barbell was born in Merchingen in 1540 and grew up with her sister Sunna in her parental home. She left home at an early age to go into service with a farmer in Esch near Trier, but returned home shortly thereafter. Far from home, her hopes had been dashed several times. She had become involved with her master's farm labourer, had become pregnant by him and subsequently lost the child her lover had not accepted. Immediately after her pregnancy had become public knowledge, Barbell was dismissed from her job without receiving the pay that she was entitled to.

She married the farmer Class Lauer. However, the rumours of her experiences far away from home did not cease. She gave birth to a girl, the couple's only child. At that time she often met with a neighbour who had to make a hasty departure from the village in 1583 because she was repeatedly accused of having practised sorcery. Barbell's sister had also married, and was living nearby with her husband, two sons and daughter. At some point the two sisters had a quarrel, whereupon Barbell uttered threats against her niece. When one of her sister's horses died, Barbell's nephew accused her of being a witch. Barbell then accused her nephew of theft and of having attempted to cut the horse's tendons. The conflict led to further threats and at one point Barbell beat her nephew. As a result, the nephew's whole body swelled up and remained in that condition for several weeks, which reinforced the suspicion of evil-doing. A neighbour accused Barbell of having caused her pain for a whole year by touching her breast on visiting her at child birth. Barbell was also held responsible for the recent sudden death of her seven-year-old son. A number of convicted people claimed Barbell was a witch. When Barbell's brother-in-law suddenly became ill, he accused her of having caused his sufferings. He died shortly after that and Barbell's incarceration seemed inevitable. It was only due to the fact that her husband bravely stood up for his wife that she was spared.

The sister continued to spread rumours and Barbell tried to dispel them through hospitality. A labourer whom Barbell had been feeding for several weeks suddenly became ill after a meal. He accused her of sorcery and died, and Barbell was taken into custody. His corpse was inspected and deemed bewitched because of its unusual appearance. Together with three other male townsmen, Barbell's nephew accused her of sorcery. Other witnesses, all males except for her sister and a neighbour, confirmed the suspicions against Barbell; among them was a farm labourer who told of an incident 13 years earlier when he had been lying ill in a barn drinking a litre of wine: just as he had finished his wine, Barbell had appeared in front of his bed, touched his jug and then his body, but was unable to cause any harm because he had blessed himself earlier that day. When tortured, Barbell named 20 accomplices, including her sister and her nephew. One month after her execution, her sister and her nephew were also burnt at the stake (Labovie 1991, pp. 155–61).

It is likely that Barbell did not leave her parental home early without reason. She barely suppressed her sexual and her aggressive feelings, which might have been a cause of fear. She had been wronged in several respects: she had been dismissed from her job without being paid, she claimed her nephew had robbed her, and the labourer had lived at her expense. The fear of Barbell's revenge and the increasing suspicion of witchcraft accusations extended over a ten-year period. She may actually have intended to seduce the farm labourer in the barn and he may have been afraid of her revenge after he rejected her. His fear was so great that even 13 years later he felt the need to destroy Barbell. Fear of Barbell's revenge obviously led to numerous psychosomatic reactions, which again were interpreted as her practice of witchcraft and increased the fear. In fact, even real illnesses – for example, in the case of the neighbour's suffering – were interpreted as Barbell's doing.

The Psychoanalysis of Witchcraft Accusations

If witchery is not damage caused by a witch but the result of psychic conflicts, where harm is the consequence of fear itself or a random occurrence that is interpreted as having been initiated by a witch, we have to analyse the unconscious psychic processes that make such a process possible. These processes were never conscious; people really believed in the existence of witches and their destructive witchery.

Aggressions against women, who were usually old and defenceless, and the refusal to provide basic assistance caused the fear of revenge. Gods and demons had always ruled people's moral life. The fear of being at the mercy of a witch's revenge was an effective deterrent of violations against the traditional norm of mutual assistance, because morally, the witches were in the right. Melanie Klein (1972, p. 52) considers the fear of being persecuted by entirely evil images as the earliest expression of conscience. The witchcraft accusations imply a conflict of the superego. The witch appears as the early superego imago.

We might consider, for example, the head of the household described by Thomas. After he rejected the woman who might have cursed him in her anger, she left. The man, however, was still afraid that she would now take revenge on him. He interpreted everything that happened from then onwards as part of her revenge. In his imagination, the woman became more and more powerful and demonical. She no longer had anything in common with the woman she had been when she knocked on his door. As far as the head of the household was concerned, she had become a witch. In Barbell's case, the witchcraft accusations dragged on for ten years, and only after numerous conflicts did she become a witch in people's imagination.

In psychoanalysis this process is known as *projective identification*. The man projects his own aggressions and feelings of persecution on to another person, in this case the old woman. The image of the witch is an imago, an internal image, containing personal aggressions. It is only after the projection of these impulses that she becomes so evil and vengeful. Since it is not a mature type of projection, where the impulse would no longer be attributed to the original person, but a very archaic type of projection, the man remains attached to his impulse, aggressions and fear of revenge. He expects aggression on the part of the woman to come at any time.

Kernberg (1967, p. 669) refers to this as an ongoing 'empathy' where fear and personal aggression continue to exist and are even enforced by the ever more threatening features of the woman. Real occurrences, now interpreted as damage caused by the woman, make the woman's features all the more menacing. The ongoing 'empathy' explains why the alleged witch was always found quickly after damage occurred, which often did not immediately follow the rejection of the woman. Witchcraft was only considered when there was already a suspect at hand.

Kernberg describes how the process of projective identification makes the object – that is, the person on to whom the accuser's own impulses are projected – become more and more of a potential threat. Finally, fear results from the urge to control such a person, whereby destruction is obviously the greatest possible form of control.

> The main purpose of projection here is to externalize the all-bad, aggressive self and object images, and the main consequence of this need is the development of dangerous, retaliatory objects against which the patient has to defend himself. This projection of aggression is rather unsuccessful ... the very intensity of the projective needs, plus the general ego weakness characterizing these patients, weakens ego boundaries in the particular area of the projection of aggression. This leads such patients to feel that they can still identify themselves with the object onto whom aggression has been projected, and their ongoing 'empathy' with the now threatening object maintains and increases the fear of their own projected aggression. Therefore, they have to control the object in order to prevent it from attacking them under the influence of the (projected) aggressive impulses; they have to attack and control the object before (as they fear) they themselves are attacked and destroyed. (Kernberg 1967, p. 669)

The idea of an increasingly threatening object assumes that the defence mechanism of splitting has taken place. Only extremely bad objects, like the image of the witch, allow strong aggression to erupt without feelings of guilt.

The process of projective identification consists of three stages or aspects. During the first stage of the process – as described above – part of the accuser's own impulses are projected on to another person and the idea emerges that these impulses control the person from within. Then pressure is exerted through interpersonal interaction inducing the recipient of the projection to feel compelled to think, experience, and act according to the projection. He or she is meant to identify with the projected impulses and feelings. After the recipient has worked out these feelings psychically, they are then reinternalised by the person projecting them (Ogden 1988, p. 2).

We have clearly identified the first part of the process, namely the projection of the accuser's own impulses. What about the second stage? Was there any interpersonal interaction between the person projecting the impulses and the recipient, whereby the former urged the other to act according to his projection? The projection has to be confirmed and for that purpose the person projecting the impulses often manipulates reality and undermines the testing of reality. He or she exerts immense pressure on the recipient in order to make the latter act according to the projection (Ogden 1988, p. 5).

This is exactly what an accuser did. He needed evidence to confirm (to himself and others) that the woman was really a witch. He manipulated such evidence by means of witches' ordeals, by trying to detect signs of witchcraft and by denunciation. However, he was still not satisfied, because a witch could not be executed for being a witch unless she confessed. Accused women had to testify that they had identified themselves with the impulse and consequently turned into witches. The confession was crucial to all witch trials. For this reason legal procedures were modified and the original purpose of torture was reversed. In fact, a witch had already been convicted before torture took place. This means that the importance of her confession can be derived only from the unconscious motivation of the accusers, who needed the confession in order to overcome their own fear and aggression. Only if the woman confessed to being a witch could the accuser be certain that his own impulses controlled the woman from within. The woman had identified herself with the projected aggressions and ideas. It seemed to be insignificant for the accuser that such confessions were made only because the woman was tortured continuously. His reality testing in this particular area was undermined. Nothing less than the destruction of the woman could reduce his aggression and fear of revenge. With the woman's execution, his projected feelings were destroyed.

During the third stage of projective identification, the projections are reintrojected. The accuser externalised the conflict which had arisen from his own immoral behaviour. Thus, he settled the conflict with people around him rather than within himself. His aggression and fear were eliminated as soon as the witch had been burned to death. Furthermore, the collective conviction of the witch – after all, she was executed by an official court – reinforced the immoral accuser's belief that he was the one acting on moral grounds since he had the court on his side. After the execution of the witch, he could regard himself as an honest person, since his aggression and fear of revenge had been legally destroyed.

Consequently, the accusation of witchcraft was based on the following unconscious dynamic: the future accuser would refuse to help a certain woman or would behave in an aggressive and immoral way. The fear of retribution developed into anxiety. The image of a witch seeking revenge is projected on to the rejected woman. Since he is bound to his own impulses through his ongoing 'empathy', the accuser still expects the woman to take revenge on him. Occurrences of harm are now interpreted as having been produced by the woman and thus increase her vengeful characteristics in the mind of the accuser. Fearing attack, the accuser himself has to go on the offensive. Consequently, the woman is accused of witchcraft. In accordance with the legal procedures of the day, she is forced to admit to being a witch. The accuser needs her confession, because only then can he be sure that she has identified herself with his own impulses and ideas. After the confession she is executed, and the accuser feels relieved and liberated from his own unpleasant impulses. The destruction of these impulses is then reintrojected. The accuser no longer feels persecuted, at least not until he again behaves in an immoral manner.

The psychic process of projective identification also explains other phenomena of the witch persecution. According to Kernberg, projective identification results in a partial weakness of the ego's boundaries. It is no longer possible to decide whether an impulse comes from within oneself or from someone else. The consequences are insufficient control of fears and impulses as well as the emergence of primary process thinking (Kernberg 1967, pp. 662–3).

All ideas concerning the witches' activities in such cases are proof of primary process thinking. For example, *maleficium* was caused by shifting to an analogous process and not by causality. According to people's beliefs, the above-mentioned milk theft could be explained as follows: a witch put a bucket between her feet and stole the milk by means of a knife that was stuck in the wall. The milk from the victim's cow came through the knife. Rain or hailstorms were explained as follows: a witch dug a pit in a field, poured water into it, and stirred it, so that it moved towards heaven. The witches' ordeals demonstrated that empirical evidence was being collected. Since they were inhabited by a light spirit, witches were believed to be lighter in weight. Therefore, they would float when subjected to trial by water, or would be discovered when subjected to trial by weight. The reality testing of the ego was so distorted that people did not realise that, in fact, there was no chance of proving one's innocence.

One has to take into consideration the fact that the accusers were otherwise capable citizens; professionals such as doctors, manual workers or farmers. It was the deficient control of fear and impulses that eventually resulted in the urge to destroy witches.

The Accused Women

The theory that discrimination or the denial of rightful claims or alms was a basis for accusing women of being witches implies that the witch must have been in a socially and economically subordinate position compared to her accuser. This explains why the majority of the accused women were very poor. According to Thomas (1979), the new economic developments – greed for landholdings, price increases, expansion of the cities and the focus on materialistic values – destroyed the tradition of mutual assistance while, at the same time, the situation of the poor population worsened dramatically. Thomas states that the denial of alms of which the accusers were guilty was an expression of the fact that the tradition of mutual assistance on which many village communities were founded was breaking down. Lending and giving away food and drink was considered to be a neighbourly duty. Borrowing materials was also a common feature of community life. The accusers knew very well that they were violating an old moral principle when they denied alms. They were aware that they were placing their own selfish interests above those of the community. According to Thomas, this deterioration of the poor people's situation contributes to the explanation of why witches were mainly women, many of them widows. They had often been deserted by their friends, were bent with age and generally suffered from various afflictions. Women ranged among the most needy members of society. People with physical defects were also suspected of witchcraft, not because of their handicaps but because they were dependent on alms as a result of their handicaps (Thomas 1979, pp. 288–98). The decisive factor for being suspected of witchcraft was not so much their appearance but rather their social situation.

Apart from the arbitrariness of denunciation, the majority of them were old women living on the fringes of society, caught, due to their social situation, in a dependent relationship to the people accusing them of witchcraft (Behringer 1986, p. 150). The motive attributed to the women played an important role in the denunciation. During the interrogations, often only the names of those women who were considered to be witches due to their low social status were written down. These names had been revealed under torture. In the sixteenth century, the economic and social situation of women had changed dramatically. As a consequence of the severe economic crisis in the sixteenth century, it was particularly elderly women, who were unable to work enough to earn a living, who were plunged into the greatest misery.

Between the thirteenth and the fifteenth centuries, women of all strata of society lived in relatively good social conditions. At that time, the production of crafted goods increased. Higher demand, a concentration of wealth and an extension of trade with other regions made craft professions, urban services and the trades more and more important. Women worked in almost all guilds and took an active interest in business life (Wolf-Graaf 1983, pp. 15-23). In thirteenth-century Paris, women were allowed to work in 86 out of 100 professions (Shahar 1983, p. 180). Noblewomen possessed hereditary feudal rights. Since the noblemen were often absent for a long time because of the many wars, the women had to look after the family's property, often for a long period of time. In the country as well as in the cities, women had to pay the same taxes and duties as men. Women could acquire civil rights and run a business on their own. However, they did not have any political rights, a fact which turned out to be very significant during the sixteenth century, when women were forced out of nearly all professions requiring particular qualifications. Women were neither allowed to occupy public positions, nor could they appear as authorised representatives in court. Only married women had the right to represent their husbands in court. As a rule, criminal proceedings could not be instituted by women.

As a result of numerous wars, women outnumbered men during the Middle Ages and during the Early Modern Age in Europe. Unmarried women of age and widows had, relatively speaking, many rights, whereas married women were subordinate to their husbands. Women who worked and lived on a farm were usually provided with food and clothes. Many of them remained unmarried. On the one hand, and in many cases, their feudal lords forbade them to marry, fearing they might have to feed even more hungry mouths; but, on the other hand, many women simply did not want to marry (Wolf-Graaf 1983, pp. 15-23). In the Early Modern Age, about 40 per cent of all women were unmarried (Ozment 1983, p. 159). Farmers tended to marry at the relatively old age of 28-30 years, if at all (Dülmen 1982, p. 200). Girls from wealthy families were usually married at the age of 13, whereas their husbands were between 27 and 31 years old (Shahar 1983, p. 171).

In the Middle Ages and the Early Modern Age, many unmarried men and women lived in monasteries and convents or in other religious communities. The best known among these communities were definitely the Beguines. They spread all over Europe in the twelfth and thirteenth centuries. Many unmarried women lived in Beguine communities or shared houses and earned their living by pursuing regular work. Modesty, solidarity and religious devotion were among their objectives. Their writings were couched in colloquial language and emphasised the relationship of each individual to God, Jesus and the Virgin Mary. Although, in 1216, the Pope still recognised the Beguines as a religious community, in 1311 he accused them of heresy. As a result, they were prohibited and subsequently persecuted (Wolf-Graaf 1983, pp. 50–60).

It was not until the severe economic crisis in the sixteenth century that this situation radically changed. Women were increasingly excluded from the guilds. Many small businesses of master craftsmen were no longer competitive and became suppliers for other, more prosperous craft businesses. Journeymen now began to produce partial products or finished goods at home. They received raw materials and a certain price for each unit delivered.

Due to growing poverty in the countryside, peasants were no longer able to go into the city in order to sell their goods. The merchants gave them raw materials and bought the goods locally at lower prices. Craftsmen in the cities faced the growing pressure of competition. Women in the countryside were increasingly dependent on the merchants. The cottage industry, once an additional income, became more and more time-consuming and less lucrative. After the Thirty Years' War (1618–1648), manufactories came into existence. The development of new and larger working tools as well as the increasing division of work into individual work processes paved the way for inhuman working conditions and for exploitation.

Women in particular were ousted from urban trades and performed only unskilled work in manufactories and for the merchants (Wolf-Graaf 1983, pp. 72–82). With the emergence of these new working structures in the sixteenth century, the situation of women changed drastically. Expulsion from the guilds, where they had enjoyed more or less equal rights, meant that they were forced into the exploitative working conditions of manufactories and cottage industries. Only younger women could cope with these working conditions, while older ones could no longer find work and were thus dependent on begging or other means of support. The situation was aggravated by the severe economic crisis in the sixteenth century, which led to the impoverishment of large sections of the population. The majority of those in need could no longer be provided for by the old system of neighbourly help.

As a consequence of the severe economic crisis, the number of beggars and vagrants – a group that included many women and children – rose to a threatening level, and bands of robbers made the roads unsafe (Dülmen 1982, pp. 226–34). The itinerant people were a motley group, in no way homogeneous, who moved from place to place. Artists, jugglers, veterans, journeymen, pilgrims, pedlars, gypsies and beggars were included in this group.

In the second half of the sixteenth century, harsh punishment and prosecution were used to control vagrancy and robbery. In 1536, every beggar in England who was able to work was whipped. If they continued to beg, their right ear was cut off. If they were caught begging a third time, they were sentenced to death (Attali 1981, p. 91).

Finally, in the seventeenth century, these vagrants were put into Poor Houses and forced to perform labour service. Among these were many women and children (Wolf-Graaf 1983, p. 105).

It can be seen that women were especially affected by the economic changes, changes which contributed significantly to the impoverishment of older women in particular. They lived in a state of legal and social uncertainty and consequently became more and more dependent on the support of others, support that could no longer be provided because of the general economic crisis, increasing poverty and the individual pursuit of property.

From the above we can say in conclusion that the fear of being bewitched was the actual reason for the witch trials. It can only be understood by looking at the psychic situation of the accusers, and it is closely connected with the social impoverishment of a large proportion of the female population. The willingness to fear the revenge of women might have been increased by the fact that the social changes took place at their expense. Women who were convicted of witchcraft often believed in witches, but they did not think of themselves as witches, except for those who confirmed the suspicion under torture.

" Though there were women who confessed to being a witch or a she-devil even without being tortured, as well as women who had many years of experience with magic and were on trial for that reason, most men and women sentenced to death on the grounds of using witchcraft had hardly had any experience with non-Christian magical practices. Under torture they thus reproduced only widespread notions that corresponded to what the theologically learned jurists wanted to hear. (Dülmen 1987, p. 130)

Those who were convicted of witchcraft had no characteristic features in common which would have marked them as witches, except for their low rank in society and the fact that they were women.

3 The Fear of Witches

God and the Devil, the Virgin Mary and the Witch

In order to understand people's fear of witches, we have to take a closer look at sixteenth- and seventeenth-century cosmology and the place witches occupied within it. With the development of urban culture in the twelfth and thirteenth centuries, the cult of the Virgin Mary developed into a phenomenon that affected many people. The Virgin was a popular theme in art and literature and the cult reached its peak around the fifteenth century. The Madonna was the most powerful of the saints. Her support as the mother of Jesus was considered infallible and her help was effective. Hers was the object of a rapturous cult. Everything from her milk to her hair was an object of worship, as well as her protective cloak which she cast about her ever more graciously (Romano and Tenenti 1967, p. 241). In the sixteenth and seventeenth centuries, relics were still worshipped in various churches. Looking at them, and after paying a certain sum of money, worshippers were spared a number of years of purgatory. The relic collection in Wittenberg consisted of one hair and a drop of milk from the Virgin Mary (Erikson 1975, p. 191). People also brought their worldly worries, pledges for protection and good health before her. They sought her help through donations, confessions, prayers and submission. The world of belief was split into 'all good' and 'all bad' idealised objects. On the one hand, there was the fear of the evil woman, the witch, who brought disease and infertility; on the other, the Virgin Mary was asked to bestow mercy and health. The interplay of these extremes characterises the sixteenth and seventeenth centuries (cf. Chapters 5 and 6).

There was another figure, in addition to the Virgin Mary and the witch, which was prominent in people's imaginations: the Devil. It was around the fourteenth century that the Devil, once a fallen angel, became the absolute antagonist to God, a kind of anti-God. Accordingly, his appearance was the complete opposite to God's. He was a black man with horns. His body was a cross between that of a man and that of a goat. His hands and feet had fingers and toes, but they were all of equal length and ended in sharp claws. His voice sounded horrible and discordant, his articulation was poor, and his face always exhibited a gloomy, morose expression. His lower body was ugly, dirty and foul-smelling (Zacharias 1970, pp. 57–66).

The Devil was worshipped on the sabbath, as has already been described. From the fourteenth century onwards, the sabbath took on the form of a reverse mass, the black mass (Michelet 1974, p. 99). The altar was covered with an old ugly cloth, upon which some images of the Devil, in the form of goblets, hosts and urns, were placed. The Devil's urine was used as holy water. The ritual began with denouncing God and worshipping the Devil. The kiss on the Devil's rear found its counterpart not only in the mediaeval feudal kiss but also in the kiss of peace in the Christian mass. The initiation with the witches' mark corresponded to baptism and confirmation. Communion was taken in the form of a wafer imprinted with the Devil's likeness which was hard to swallow, together with a foul-tasting liquid. In contrast to the hosts used in Christian mass, these were black in colour, hence the name 'black mass'. The Devil held a sermon, heard confessions and the queen of the witches' sabbath sat next to Satan in analogy to the Virgin Mary sitting next to God. Sacrificial offerings were also brought before the Devil. They danced the sabbath round dance with their backs toward the inside of the circle. The sign of the cross was made with the left hand while invoking various Devils.

Sexual intercourse with the Devil was described as uncomfortable and painful. His member was said to have scales and to be particularly cold (Zacharias 1970, p. 58). Zacharias sees the sexual practices advocated by the Devil, particularly homosexuality and incest, as counterparts to the Christian Agape, or spiritual love. These were the images that people in the early modern age entertained of Devil worship at the sabbath (Zacharias 1970, p.32).

The Devil was considered omnipotent. It was only through his help that witches were able to acquire magical powers. He subjugated the witches through the so-called pact with the Devil. The idea that witches could fly and do harm, thanks to their pact with the Devil and the fact that they were his paramours, developed in the late thirteenth century. The idea of a nightly witches' meeting, the witches' sabbath, was first documented only during the witch trials around 1600 (Dülmen 1987, p. 128).

Popular imagination underwent a complete change during the fourteenth and fifteenth centuries to become a set of completely different ideas and images. These consisted of the good, asexual images of God and the Virgin Mary, and the evil images of the unbridled sexual energy of the witch and the Devil. This splitting into good and evil powers has to be understood as the expression of a psychic process. Images of witches and the Devil have always existed, but the content of these images has been subject to change, which is a reflection of psychic transformation.

There was magic which could be used against witches and demons. A person could beat a witch by putting his hat on the ground and beating it with a hazelnut stick that had been cut while pronouncing magical incantations. There were various means of protection against milk magic: for example, dipping hot steel into the milk (Labovie 1987, p. 72).

The mediaeval Devil had completely different features compared to those of the early modern age. The mediaeval Devil was gullible, and could be tricked with a little peasant cunning. The Devil of the early modern age became a persecutory threat to existence (Hammes 1977, p. 154). Why, then, did the belief in the power of protective magic fail?

The Psychogenesis of the Notion of Witches and the Devil

One prerequisite for accusations of witchcraft was that images were either good or absolutely bad. From a psychoanalytical perspective, this process can be seen as the defence mechanism of splitting. According to Melanie Klein (1972, p. 45), the earliest memories of a small child at the mother's breast are split as the child cannot yet see the mother as an integral person, but only as separate objects (good and bad breast). Klein refers to this as a paranoid-schizoid position. Images of the mother are developed and provided with the child's own emotions, for example, aggressions, known as 'imagines'. These early 'imagines' can change very quickly from good to bad and vice versa, just as satisfaction follows hunger and the perception of the child changes.

Margaret Mahler's (1975, p. 1086) hypothesis is that there are children who fail to reconcile in the rapprochement stage of the separation and individuation process after the symbiosis with the mother, and whose emotional 'reloading' and reassurance with the mother is interrupted. These children are unable to overcome the splitting of these imagines into the categories of absolutely good and absolutely bad. Under these circumstances, an bad image filled with individual aggressions is developed which itself is a basis for a relatively sustained splitting of the world of imagination into good and bad.

New findings in the area of infant research (Dornes 1993; 1997, pp. 171–3) support the theory that during normal development, an infant has the capability of integration very early on, whereas object splitting, even at this time, occurs as a type of defence mechanism. Splitting is a mechanism actively employed by the ego to help prevent anxiety. If the process of integrating good and bad experiences does not succeed, fears of persecution by absolute evil images develop. The image of the good, providing mother has to be protected against the destructive power of the bad, punitive and depriving mother. Thus, these two have to be split as radically as possible. The good images are important for the further psychic development of a person, because only they can support integration and positive self-concept. The diametrically opposed images must be actively kept apart at all times, because if not, they could lead to extreme fear of the destructive power of the bad images and thus a fear of one's own aggressions contained in these images.

We might view the witch as an imago of the bad mother. The witch harms people, has an evil mind and kills children. Her oral-aggressive character is expressed in the tale of Hansel and Gretel in the form of the child-devouring witch. It is also expressed in the images of people in the early modern age. Stealing milk was one of the major accusations against witches. The witch is the image of the depriving, frustrating mother bearing the aggressions of the child who felt this aggression while experiencing these frustrations. This image was projected on to women in the witchcraft accusations already described.

I personally was forced to experience the image of a witch as a very early, negative image of a mother, during my work as a teacher at a school for emotionally disturbed children. It was a custom in my class of 14 very aggressive boys aged between 12 and 14, to trade their belongings in the morning: a sandwich for a soft drink; toys for a notebook. Very often, the pupils tried to include the milk I distributed every morning after the break, something I had strictly prohibited. I allowed them to trade things, but not their milk. Each pupil was to drink his own milk. This rule was necessary because much of the trading was based on blackmail, and I wanted to prevent a situation in which some pupils would not have any milk at all.

When I entered the classroom one morning after the break, I noticed that it had already been unlocked by a colleague. I saw that one pupil, a specialist in blackmail, had the milk packages for the whole class piled up on his desk. I was angered by this obvious disregard for my rule, took the milk packages and put them back on my table, taking advantage of the fact that not all the pupils were back in the room yet. To strengthen my position, I stood in front of my desk, and then the battle began. As expected, the pupil began to shout insults at me: he said that I should give him back the milk the others had given to him of their own free will.

To my surprise, the whole class made a common cause against me now, something that had never happened before. All of them loudly insisted that it was true: they had given him the milk voluntarily. Then I wanted to know what had made them give it away. In great excitement, the boy told me that his mother was expecting a baby and that the baby would need lots of milk. The milk was intended for his mother so the baby would grow well. I was to give him back the milk immediately, or the baby would die. 'And that would be your fault', he shouted. The atmosphere in the classroom rapidly became a united front of hatred against me. And then I heard from another corner: 'You witch, you!' At this point, I could hardly keep the boys in their seats. After I had understood the reason, I was able to verbalise the conflict and so harmony was restored. The pupils had identified themselves with the unborn baby, and I had become the evil mother who wanted to kill it. After I was able to make it clear to them that the baby would not die, that its well-being was very important to me and that I cared very much that every one of them got his milk too, they could calm down and drink their milk. The image of the child-killing, milk-stealing witch had changed back to that of the good mother. The early self and object images can change very quickly.

The conflict with my class shows the superego conflict contained within the witchcraft accusation. The pupil had broken my law. He had my revenge and aggression to fear. The archaic superego, a forerunner to the superego, is based on submission and fear of revenge.

The witch is basically the hated, depriving mother, hence the serious accusations of harmful magic, the destruction of the harvest and the theft of milk. It is primarily the oral image of the mother which is divided into the witch, on the one hand, and, on the other, the protective, helpful Virgin Mary, a drop of whose milk can save someone a certain number of years of purgatory. The mother is always female, hence the predominant projection of the witch image on to women. The image of the witch corresponds to the reversal of the idealisation of the Virgin Mary. The one is young, the other old.

Apart from the aspect of the oral mother, the image of the witch also consists of the aspects of the oedipal mother. The image of the oedipally threatening mother is reinforced by that of the dangerous pregenital mother. Historically, the witch trials were centred around accusations of harmful magic and later began to focus more and more on the accusations of having intercourse with the Devil. Through the domination of the splitting mechanisms, the oedipal strivings are split off and projected on to the image of the Devil. Mary's virginity protects people against incestuous, oedipally centred sexual impulses and fears. The Devil who has intercourse with a witch gains power and domination through his sexuality.

This splitting mechanism is supported by processes such as primitive idealisation (Kernberg 1967, p. 668). The Virgin Mary could thus take over the function of idealised imagines and protect against incestuous fears. In addition to projective identification, the mechanisms of the witchcraft accusations, we can also observe a third process at work which accompanies this splitting, that of omnipotence and devaluation. At times, protection is sought from magically elevated and idealised persons; at other times, there is the feeling of power in oneself and potency. The Devil does not submit to God: he sticks to his own claim of omnipotence (Leber 1983, p. 133).

According to Freud, the Devil is a figure upon which to project repressed impulses: 'In our eyes, the demons are bad and reprehensible wishes, derivatives of instinctual impulses that have been repudiated and repressed. We merely eliminate the projection of these mental entities into the external world which the middle ages carried out; instead, we regard them as having arisen in the patient´s inernal life, where they have their abode' (Freud 1923b, p. 72).

In his work on 'A Seventeenth-Century Demonological Neurosis', Freud (1923b) analyses the history of the illness of the painter, Christoph Haitzmann, who, in 1669, gave his soul to the Devil for nine years. Experiencing visions and suffering from epileptic fits, he went on a pilgrimage to Mariazell in order to be released from his pact with the Devil through the intervention of the Virgin Mary of Mariazell. The pact written in blood was given back to him, but the symptoms returned shortly after his recovery.

The Devil came to the painter first in the guise of an honourable citizen, but then he began to acquire more and more sexual features:

> On the first occasion, as I have mentioned, he saw the Evil One in shape of an honest citizen. But already on the second occasion the Devil was naked and misshapen, and had two pairs of female breasts. In none of his subsequent apparitions are the breasts absent, either as a single or a double pair. Only in one of them does the Devil exhibit, in addition to the breasts, a large penis ending in a snake. (Freud 1923b, p. 89)

Freud sees the Devil as a direct father substitute. The longing for the father is ambivalent: there is a tender, submissive, attitude towards him, but also hostility. God and the Devil were originally identical, one single figure, which was later split into two opposing characteristics, mirroring the ambivalence which dominates the individual personal relationship to one's own father. The father is the individual archetype of God and the Devil, according to Freud.

The Devil's image also reflects the ambitions of the painter himself. According to Freud, the breasts are an expression of the painter's feminine attitude toward his father, which has its climax in the fantasy of bearing him a child (nine years of submission). The feminine attitude is then repressed as a consequence of the threat of castration. Freud does not forget that the breasts might be the expression of a strong fixation on the mother and the tenderness that is projected from mother to father, which in turn is responsible for the hostility towards the father. The painter may be one of the types 'who are known as "eternal sucklings" – who cannot tear themselves away from the blissful situation at the mother's breast, and who, all through their lives, persist in a demand to be nourished by someone else' (Freud 1923b, p. 104).

Freud analyses the oral fixation on the mother and emphasises the Devil as a father substitute. The emphasis on the father substitute is based on a mistranslation, probably by Freud, stating that the death of the father is the triggering situation for the Devil neurosis. The sources read *ex morte parentis* (Freud 1923b, p. 81), which translates as 'death of the parents' and not 'death of the father'. The triggering situation was the death of his parents, not the father alone.

It is astonishing that Freud neglects the aspect of libidinal wishes, which the painter can only express with the help of the Devil. Freud describes three phases of the painter's visions:

" First, temptation appeared in the form of a finely dressed cavalier, who tried to persuade him to throw away the document attesting his admission to the Brotherhood of the Holy Rosary. He resisted this temptation, whereupon the same thing happened next day; only this time the scene was laid in a magnificently decorated hall in which grand gentlemen were dancing with beautiful ladies ... After he had made this vision disappear by prayer, it was repeated once more a few days later, in a still more pressing form. This time the cavalier sent one of the most beautiful of the ladies who sat at the banqueting table to him to persuade him to join their company, and he had difficulty in defending himself from the temptress ... The same person who had so often made proposals to him now approached him and summoned him to ascend the throne, for they 'wanted to have him for their King and to honour him for ever'. This extravagant phantasy concluded the first, perfectly transparent, phase of the story of this temptation.

" There was bound to be a revulsion against this. An ascetic reaction reared its head. On October 20 a great light appeared, and a voice came from it, making itself known as Christ, and commanded him to forswear this wicked world and serve God in the wilderness for six years. The painter clearly suffered more from these holy apparitions than from the earlier demoniacal ones; ... There than appeared, instead of Christ, the Holy Mother herself, who, reminding him of what she had already done on his behalf, called on him to obey the command of her dear Son. 'Since he could not truly resolve so to do', Christ appeared to him again the next day and upbraided him soundly with threats and promises. At last he gave way and made up his mind to leave the world and to do what was required of him. With this decision, the second phase ended ... Nevertheless, his resolution cannot have been firm enough or he must have delayed its execution too long; for while he was in the midst of his devotions, on December 26, in St. Stephen's Cathedral, catching sight of a strapping young woman accompanied by a smartly dressed gentleman, he could not fend off the thought that he might himself be in this gentleman's place. This called for punishment, and that very evening it overtook him like a thunderbolt. He saw himself in bright flames and sank down in a swoon. Attempts werde made to rouse him but he rolled about in the room till blood flowed from his mouth and nose. He felt that he was surrounded by heat and noisome smells, and he heard a voice say that he had been condemned to this state of punishment for his vain and idle thoughts. Later he was scourged with ropes by Evil Spirits, and was told that he would be tormented like this every day until he had decided to enter the Order of Anchorites. (Freud 1923b, pp. 100–2)

The visions of the Devil involved: first, the seduction phantasy and the painter's sexual and oedipal strivings; second, the defence of the strivings through submission to the ascetic Virgin Mary; and finally, punishment through divine forces.

" They consisted in visions and 'absences', in which he saw and experienced every kind of thing, in convulsive seizures accompanied by the most painful sensations, on one occasion in paralysis of the legs, and so on. This time, however, it was not the Devil who tormented him; it was by sacred figures that he was vexed – by Christ and by the Blessed Virgin herself. It is remarkable that he suffered no less through these heavenly manifestations and the punishments they inflicted on him than he had formerly through his traffic with the Devil. (Freud 1923b, p. 77)

In the painter's possession, the defence at times gained control of the ego, that is, submission to the idealised, ascetic Virgin and the punitive Christ, or the Devil and the painter's libidinal wishes, which were being defended. The Devil enabled the painter to express his libidinal wishes and activated oedipal strivings as well as fantasies of omnipotence. The oedipal strivings were immediately suppressed, rather than being resolved through competition and identification with the father. As the internalisation of the incest taboo, they were defended in form of an avoidance of the oedipal situation (the ascetic solution).

While the witch is the imago of the oral-aggressive, threateningly incestuous, evil mother, the Devil appears as a projection of the painter's own fantasies of sexual omnipotence. The question which arises is why impulses and affects in the Early Modern Age could only be defended by extreme splitting processes and submission. In Chapter 7, I will follow up on the question of oedipal development and possession in the Early Modern Age.

Childhood in the Early Modern Age

If we are to understand the image of a witch in a psychodynamic sense as an expression of an extreme splitting mechanism, then we must examine the living conditions of children in the Early Modern Age. Even so, we have to bear in mind that the excess of oral aggression which is held responsible for the splitting mechanism (Klein 1972, pp. 106–10; Kernberg 1975, p. 41), cannot in itself provide an explanation for a historical phenomenon.

However much disparity there may be between the findings of individual researchers on the history of childhood, they are in agreement on one point: in the Early Modern Age there was a fundamental change in the attitude of parents towards their children. The concept of childhood was subject to far-reaching changes. According to Ariès (1975), childhood was only 'discovered' in the sixteenth century. Prior to this, there was no physical or cultural separation of children and adults. Children were included in adult activities from an early age. The exclusion of children from adult life, which stemmed from the sixteenth century, was generally accepted in the seventeenth century and manifested itself in the form of clothes specially designed for children, the invention of special toys and the tendency for children to go to special institutions for education. This is portrayed by Ariès as a situation in which children moved from the freedom and casualness they enjoyed in a holistic world into one of pedagogical conditioning in a society which aimed increasingly to subdivide and institutionalise all areas of life.

Ariès' interpretation contradicts the results of psycho-historical research by deMause and his research group (1974). Although they also concluded that childhood was not treated as a sphere of life in its own right until the sixteenth century, they consulted different sources and thus arrived at completely different conclusions:

" The history of childhood is a nightmare, from which we are just now awakening. The further we go back in history, the more unsatisfactory was the care of children, and the greater the likelihood that children would be killed, abandoned, beaten, tormented and sexually abused. (deMause 1974, p. 1)

The custom of handing children over to a wet nurse or foster mother spread in urban areas and, by the end of the seventeenth century, this had become common practice for all sectors of urban society (Marvick 1974, p. 266; Badinter 1984). A clear distinction should be made between the fostermothers and wet nurses in the Early Modern Age and the previously common practice of childcare by wet nurses. There had always been wet nurses, but only for the ruling classes, and the wet nurses normally lived in the house; thus they were more like nannies and looked after their protégés throughout the whole of their childhood (McLaughlin 1974, pp. 115–17). The wet nurse therefore had previously been a good substitute for the physiological mother. However, the same could not be said of the new tradition of the wet nurse in the Early Modern Age.

There were three methods of choosing a fostermother and wet nurse. Either she was carefully chosen before the child's birth, which was only possible for the uppermost stratum of society, or the choice was left to chance or to an agency. The latter method became increasingly popular. The first agency was founded in Paris as far back as the thirteenth century. The more widespread the practice of giving children to wet nurses became, the further away children were sent. It was more expensive for them to live in or around the towns. The conditions of transport were catastrophic. Depending on the season, 5-15 per cent of infants died en route:

" One agent took six babies in a little cart and fell asleep, not noticing when one baby fell out and was crushed to death. Another, entrusted with seven infants, lost one so completely that no one was ever able to find out what happened to it. One old woman found herself with three newborn babies, and did not know what to do with them. (Badinter 1984, p. 94)

When children returned to the parental home, which had become unfamiliar to them, they had to compete with their own brothers and sisters, half-brothers, half-sisters and cousins for the parents' attention. Children lived with their parents up to the age of around seven or nine. In the towns, it was at this point that institutional education began. Here, particular emphasis was placed on obedience and discipline. Classrooms were run on a regime of fear and beatings (Ross 1974, pp. 197–9).

The children of manual workers were sent to other families as apprentices. Everyone, no matter how rich, sent his children to another household to work (Tucker 1974, p. 250). In the new household, just as in the parental home, children were to learn respect and obsequiousness. Children were to be dressed in simple clothes and to be hardened. They were often given very little to eat in order to make them tougher. At mealtimes, for example, they were often obliged to stand and eat leftovers:

" They should get tough meat so they will not bolt their food, and till the age of twenty they should stand during meals, while one child reads aloud to them. They should not sleep for more than six or eight hours. (Ross 1974, p. 205)

The reason that parents once again turned their children over to other people was allegedly for them to learn better manners. Tucker (1974, p. 249) challenges this and believes it was for purely pragmatic reasons. It was easier to be waited on by other people's children; they could be given worse food and denied any comfort. Had the children really been sent to learn better manners, then, Tucker argues, the parents would have made an effort to bring their children home after the apprenticeship was completed. However, they very seldom did so (Tucker 1974, pp. 250–1).

Townschildren in the Early Modern Age had three difficult physical and emotional adjustments to make. First they were handed over to the wet nurse and foster mother; then they returned to their own emotionally estranged family, and finally they had to leave home again to do an apprenticeship or to work (Ross 1974, p. 215). Badinter refers to this as a triple betrayal of the child. The child would spend five or six years in the parental home at most:

" The child of a master merchant or a master artisan, like the child of a magistrate or a court aristocrat, would typically spend long stretches of time alone, sometimes suffering lack of care and was often the victim of severe psychological and emotional neglect. (Badinter 1984, p. 91)

In the sixteenth and seventeenth centuries, we may observe an attitude of parents towards their children which is indicative of the tendency to give their children away. This does not mean that there was no parental love at this time. Arnold (1980, pp. 78–86), Pollock (1983, p. 96) and Ozment (1983, p. 171) give numerous examples of evidence of parents caring for their children. DeMause (1974, p. 51) labels the sixteenth and seventeenth centuries an age of ambivalence. Both parental attitudes co-existed, whereby the origins of the system of wet nurses as a whole has so far only been explained, most unsatisfactorily, by the hardly surprising lack of close ties between mother and child, given the fact that child mortality was as high as 20–30 per cent (Marvick 1974, p. 283).

In the sixteenth century, the state increasingly took children into care. Orphanages were built in towns. Laws were enacted to punish wet nurses and teachers for infanticide and there were more severe penalties for non-observance of these laws (Arnold 1980, pp. 43–58; Dülmen 1991). Whereas in England and Italy there was only one prosecution per year for infanticide between 1265 and 1413, prosecutions spread like wildfire in the sixteenth to eighteenth centuries (Dülmen 1991, pp. 52–7). Prosecutions for infanticide in the sixteenth and seventeenth centuries almost exclusively concerned the children's mothers, never their fathers. Unmarried mothers were treated in a particularly cruel way. They could be faced with a death penalty of beheading, drowning or being buried alive (Piers 1976, p. 422). As already mentioned, 40 per cent of women were unmarried at this time (Ozment 1983, p. 159).

Children's living conditions within society were characterised by poverty and the fight for survival. Gruel, a mixture of cow's or goat's milk, wheat and soaked bread crumbs, led to numerous stomach problems and not uncommonly to the child's death (Hunt 1970, p. 113). The child was fed when it suited the wet nurse's or mother's work schedule, not when the child was hungry. Sometimes he or she did not have enough to eat, sometimes too much. Common effects of this were heartburn, flatulence, colic, cramps, fever, green diarrhoea or constipation (Badinter 1984, p. 96). As in previous centuries, babies were given opium, liquor or spirits to keep them quiet (deMause 1974, p. 36; Badinter 1984, p. 96). In some cases, breastfeeding stopped very abruptly, sometimes with the aid of very unpleasant deterrents. Mustard, aloe or other foul-tasting substances were smeared onto the mother's nipple (Marvick 1974, p. 276). According to Hunt (1970, p. 119), children suffered from massive oral deprivation. Only the most orally aggressive children could survive.

Another cause of discomfort and illness among babies was the custom of swaddling them. First, the baby was dressed in a rough shirt that was gathered or folded several times. A nappy was wrapped around that, the child's arms were pressed against the breast and a ribbon was pulled through under its shoulders, which restricted arm and leg movement. Then the clothing and ribbons were folded between the thighs, and the whole thing was tied together from head to foot as tightly as possible with a ribbon that ran all the way round. The babies frequently had red lines, bruises and, since the nappies were not changed regularly, this led to sores and scrofulous blisters. Moreover, there was a lack of basic hygiene (Badinter 1984, p. 97). Children were swaddled for about a year, although their arms were freed up to the age of four months (Hunt 1970, p. 127).

In the sixteenth and seventeenth centuries, there was no hygiene as we know it today. This did not begin to exist until the eighteenth century (deMause 1974, p. 39). There were still no toilets in the sixteenth and seventeenth centuries. There were chamber pots, but their contents were simply emptied on to the street. The streets stank of excrement: there were human and animal excretions in every corner. A foul stench filled the whole town. In the houses too, where pets also lived, there was excrement on the floors (Marvick 1974, p. 271). The lax attitude of people towards cleanliness did not mean, however, that adults took no interest in the contents of their children's intestines. According to Hunt (1970, p. 143), adults were afraid their children would not excrete their faeces. Suppositories, enemas or oral laxatives were regularly administered, regardless of whether the child was sick or healthy. This was even begun immediately after a baby's birth. Rectal examinations were commonplace. Excrement was examined for symptoms of disease, impurities and the presence of inner demons. The child's autonomy was also greatly suppressed with beatings. Absolute obedience was the top priority for bringing up a child. Children were whipped from a very early age (deMause 1974, pp. 40–42; Hunt 1970, p. 134), often from the age of only two years. The will of a child was equated with Christian original sin. It was intolerable for children to express their own wishes. Hunt (1970, p. 134) gives examples of parents refusing children food they asked for. Requests for special clothing were dealt with in a similar fashion. The response to disobedience was normally a beating. Tales of demons and other ghouls were intended to frighten children.

DeMause (1974, p. 70) points out, however, that, contrary to previous centuries, in the Renaissance period, adults were advised for the first time to restrict the indiscriminate beating of children and only to strike them when this was justified. On the same point, Ozment (1983, p. 166) notes that in the sixteenth and seventeenth centuries, methods of upbringing were aimed at creating a religious, obedient and educable child. Strict external discipline was intended to give the child a sense of self-discipline. The aim was free inner self-control. It was believed that in order to achieve this, too much discipline was better than too little.

It is very difficult to describe the child's development during the oedipal phase, since there is little reference to this topic in the various sources (deMause 1974, p. 43). It is safe to say that, in general, sexuality was practised considerably more openly than nowadays. Children slept in the same room and often even in the same bed as adults and consequently, they were aware of sexual activities from an early age. There was no privacy: intimacies were not concealed (Hunt 1970, p.165). Children's sexual remarks were not suppressed: the struggle against masturbation did not begin until the eighteenth century. It was much more important to protect the child from sexual advances by adults. Children have been sexually abused time and again throughout history. It was not until the sixteenth and seventeenth centuries that a campaign against the sexual abuse of children began (deMause 1974, p. 43).

Children bore witness to the graphic suppression of various forms of illicit sexuality. DeMause (1974, p. 14) describes how parents particularly liked to take their children with them to hangings and other public punishments. Thus it was made clear to them that sexuality was only tolerated within certain limits. Various penalties are documented in the *Schriftenreihe des mittelalterlichen Kriminalmuseums* in Rothenburg ob der Tauber (1984, pp. 304–23): burning or hanging of both the person and the animal for sodomy; and the stocks, the birch or prison for adultery. Threats of castration were an integral part of the educational process (Marvick 1974, p. 277).

The age of seven marked the passing of childhood. Children were then given adult clothing. Dress was considered to be an important symbol of social status (Hunt 1970, p. 180). At this age the children usually left home again. They were forced to give up oedipal desires when they moved to another family and were given adult status. Sublimation of instincts was replaced by external circumstances.

The circumstances of children in the sixteenth and seventeenth centuries help us to understand the traumas of their psychic development, their heightened oral aggressions and fears related to sexuality and incest. However, these circumstances alone cannot explain the exaggerated fear of witches.

4   The Early Modern Age

Society

" Seldom is an explanation given as to why the modern era with its humanism, its rational and scientific thinking should produce these systematic mass murders. (Wolf-Graaf 1983, p. 145).

Why did the belief in protective magic fail in the Early Modern Age? Why did the fear of witches become so strong – particularly in the Early Modern Age, a period of tremendous social changes – that it led to the massacre of so many women?

The sixteenth century was marked by extreme economic crises. Women in particular were driven out of professional work and forced into cottage industries and manufacturing. There has been considerable speculation about the causes of this economic upheaval in the sixteenth century, but so far, no satisfactory explanation has been found. According to Wolf-Graaf (1983, pp. 72–82), in the sixteenth century most markets had already been opened for the selling of goods, which led to a stagnation in production. In addition, there were major changes in the channels of distribution in long-distance trade. The discovery of America in 1492 and of the sea route to India led to a shift in external markets. The main focus of long-distance trade was transferred to Portugal. For Germany, this entailed high additional costs.

Like Wolf-Graaf, Dülmen (1982, p. 38) sees the cause of the economic problems in the critical selling situation. In his view, this had been caused by over-production and over-speculation. As the second most important reason, Dülmen (1982, pp. 31–2) as well as Wolf-Graaf (1983, p. 72) mention increased grain prices. During the sixteenth century, grain prices rose disproportionately with respect to the salary of craftsmen. The increasing gap between grain prices and salaries led to the impoverishment of the vast majority of the population. The feudal lords increased their demands, while incredible sums were spent on the exorbitant running of the courts.

Dülmen (1982, p. 29) also mentions a third reason as a possible cause. Large amounts of silver and gold were being brought from America to Europe, which resulted in inflation. The value of money declined while the prices of goods and services rose. In this context, Romano and Tenenti (1967, pp. 31-6) point out that not only gold and silver but also many luxury items were brought to Europe from the recently discovered lands. These items were cheaper than those produced in the cities of Europe.

European expansion and the development of a global market were important conditions for the shift from feudalism to capitalism. According to Dülmen (1982, pp. 93-101), the exploitation of the feudal method of production, which aimed at satisfying internal demand, and the simultaneous development of a global market, are the preconditions for the beginning of the capitalist era which began in Flanders and Northern Italy during the sixteenth century. The emergence of capitalism was marked by three conditions:

- population growth, urbanisation, and a demand for mass products which could not be met by the feudal market system

- development of a global market by expanding into the New World

- a sharp increase in the amount of money in circulation.

The new economic system was favourable to the establishment of a new socio-political world order, yet it did not lead everywhere to the dissolution of the feudal system. On the contrary, in some places it strengthened tendencies towards a class-orientated hierarchical order and the centralisation of society (Dülmen 1982, pp. 10-18). Wolf-Graaf (1983, p. 15) even writes of a second period of serfdom during the sixteenth century which, however, also provoked a series of resistance movements. Between 1550 and 1650 there were countless uprisings, wars, rebellions and revolts (Dülmen 1982, p. 12).

These fundamental economic and social upheavals were accompanied by equally revolutionary changes in the society of the Early Modern Age. Knowledge, discoveries and scientific findings, brought about by Early Modern society, represented something completely new that went far beyond all previous concepts. Whereas in the Middle Ages, knowledge and erudition had been monopolised by the clergy, they now became accessible to all social classes. The educational revolution led to greater literacy and the expansion of a system of schooling. In the sixteenth century, the estimated reading public in Germany increased from 400,000 to 800,000 people. In England there were said to be between 1.5 and 2 million readers out of a population of 4 or 5 million, and by around 1600, half of the population was literate. The invention of the printing press made it possible for a book market to develop in Germany, and Luther became the first popular writer. The educational revolution was explicitly expressed in the foundation of modern science. The traditional cosmological and religious conception of the world which was based on astrology, sorcery, alchemy and the occult sciences was revolutionised by the objective and experimental sciences, which are based on experience. The most important representatives of these sciences were Galileo Galilei; Johannes Kepler; William Gilbert, who discovered magnetism; William Harvey, who discovered the circulatory system; the philosopher and poet Giordano Bruno; Francis Bacon and René Descartes (Dülmen 1982, pp. 293–306). Copernicus, Vesalius and Fracastoro also gained considerable importance (Romano and Tenenti 1967, p. 192).

The new sciences developed mainly because of the increasing need for technical knowledge which accompanied the expansion of trade. A precondition for this scientific revolution was a new attitude towards technology. From the middle of the fifteenth century onwards, the arts, which had been pejoratively called 'mechanical arts' during the Middle Ages, enjoyed tremendous popularity. The public's need for worldly education and the increasingly rapid growth of knowledge eventually contributed to the emergence of the modern sciences (Romano and Tenenti 1967, pp. 185–98).

It was only gradually that these new sciences based on reason, experience and nature became prominent. Despite their findings, many of the new scientists maintained their alchemist and astrological interpretations. Kepler was an astrologer as well as an astronomer, Comenius was both an educationalist and a pansophist (Dülmen 1982, p. 302). Kepler was fully aware of his ambiguous position and its problematic nature:

" Astrologica verily is a foolish child; but ah, what should become of her mother, the wise Astronomia, if she had this foolish daughter not? For there is more folly in the world, and this world is of such foolishness that, for her own good sake, this old prudent mother has to be beguiled by words and be deceived by her daughter's foolishness. And since Mathematicorum has such a little reward, the mother would surely have to suffer hunger if not the daughter did earn a living. (Hammes 1977, p. 17)

People were indeed afraid of the transition from the magical occult sciences to the natural sciences. Kepler's resigned words illustrate the intensity of the opposition to the new sciences: 'I think we should follow the example of the Pythagorans. We will exchange what we discover privately among ourselves while keeping silent toward the outside, so as not to die of hunger' (Hammes 1977, p. 18).

Besides the educational revolution and the emergence of empirical sciences, another revolutionary event took place in the sixteenth century, without which modernism cannot be understood: the Reformation. As early as in the fourteenth century, during the time of the papal schism, criticism of the papacy greatly increased. The fact that power and wealth were divided between the Roman curia and the worldly sovereigns caused several disputes and the faithful to become more restive (Romano and Tenenti 1967, p. 221). The existence of two Popes led to the fact that each Pope lost part of his income. However, in order to be able to imitate the extravagances of the worldly sovereigns, each Pope tried to balance his losses by increasing his income. This led to inflation within the indulgence system and a continuous increase in church taxes (Tuchman 1982, p. 301).

The indulgence system flourished until the Reformation took place. The forgiveness of sins could be bought and purgatory was now avoidable. It could be purchased for a corresponding amount of money on behalf of those already deceased (Moeller 1977, p. 55). The increase in taxes became a growing heavy burden. The clergy had to hand over about 10 per cent of their income to the Pope, Jews 20 per cent and the rest of the population 30 per cent (Romano and Tenenti 1967, p. 225).

As a reaction to this, several sects and lay religious movements emerged. They already represented the beginning of the believer's individualisation; moreover, they also contributed to the emerging doctrine of absolution for sins in the here and now. It was in order to prevent the collapse of the Church's hierarchical structure that the Inquisition began (Honegger 1977, pp. 42–3). In the sixteenth century, the decisive event finally occurred: the Reformation and, consecutively, the splitting of the universal mediaeval church into different denominations. After the proclamation of Luther's doctrines in 1517, the Protestant movement spread rapidly until 1570. This movement, however, was not uniform, and its success depended greatly on the extent to which the monarchs and nobility embraced it. It was only in 1620, when the Catholic Counter-Reformation grew more powerful, that Catholicism regained influence. In 1648, the distribution of the denominations in Europe was finally laid down. As support of the authorities was the only way to establish the reform movement, the unified state churches were created. The dependence of the Church and religion on the secular world was thus accepted.

In the course of the Counter-Reformation, even the Catholic Church had changed; its doctrines were more clearly defined; the indulgence system was prohibited; the selling of offices was no longer allowed; and strict regulations regarding monastery discipline, the observance of celibacy and the duties of the clergy were introduced.

The denominational disputes caused many people to question ecclesiastical doctrines. Priority was given to the social life of a church's members by both Churches. Every denomination became more prominent in the lives of its followers. The Christianisation of daily life was achieved. Regular attendance at services was obligatory and the rearing of children was subject to the Church's control. Church weddings were introduced and the registration of births, marriages and deaths in the parish registers became compulsory. Sexuality was regulated and the distinction between what was allowed and what was forbidden was made in accordance with the new morality. The individualisation of religion was the consequence of the Church's keen interest in its members. The Protestant movement sought salvation through acts of morality. It introduced domestic prayers and stimulated the reading of Protestant texts. The Catholic Church continued to promise salvation through ecclesiastical works. The confessional system was extended, and there was a shift from collective confessions towards individual confessions (Dülmen 1982, pp. 256–82).

The sixteenth and seventeenth centuries were clearly times of extreme social change which could not have occurred without parallel changes in the psychic structure of people at that time.

The Drives and the Ego

Together with the profound economic and social changes of the sixteenth and seventeenth centuries, interpersonal relations and people's attitudes towards themselves also changed. The early sixteenth century marked a drastic change in the individual's balance of affects and drives. The affects and drives were suddenly subjected to considerable shaping and modelling. In this respect, particular value was attached to individual self-control, which meant the exercise of self-discipline independent of external control.

It had been a custom in the Middle Ages to eat meat with one's fingers. Moreover, people shared bowls, glasses, pots and plates when eating and drinking. Stricter constraints were imposed on these eating habits in the sixteenth century. The upper classes at least began to use forks. If people did not possess a fork, they were advised to hold meat with three fingers only and not with the whole hand. It was considered improper to pounce upon food like a glutton. People were advised to wash their hands before eating. The handling of the knife also became subject to certain rules; for example, it was to be handed to another person only in a certain way.

A similar development can be seen with respect to the clearing of the nose and to spitting. Prior to the sixteenth century, when clearing their noses, people had solely been advised to be careful that what came out of their noses did not land on the table. At that time, however, the use of handkerchiefs was introduced. During the Middle Ages, spitting was a common practice that was virtually unrestricted. In the sixteenth century, it had become very important to tread out what had been spat on to the floor (Elias 1978, pp. 84–129).

The lack of concern about controlling the drives in the Middle Ages was also evident from how people relieved themselves. This was done openly in the street, in rooms, in corridors or wherever a person happened to be. Although, in the fourteenth century, chamber pots did become popular, the contents were simply emptied out of the window into the street. It was from the sixteenth century onwards that people began to behave according to certain rules. They were then expected to answer the call of nature only in places specially intended for the purpose (Kunze 1987, pp. 54–5).

Numerous descriptions of excessive feasts are also evidence of people's limited control over their drives during the Middle Ages. In public taverns, five or six courses of cooked dishes were considered a modest everyday meal; a dinner with meat also included boiled or preserved fish as well as fried or baked fish. This would be served with two different kinds of suitable wines and finished off with cheese and fruit, but not with sweets. Everyone drank wine in abundance – at least seven goblets per meal (Kunze 1987, pp. 73–6).

The aristocracy had even more sumptuous meals. During the Middle Ages, official banquets consisted of at least 30 lavishly prepared courses. People ate and drank until they fell unconscious. Often they indulged to such an extent that they had to take laxatives afterwards or needed blood-letting (Tuchmann 1982, pp. 225, 282, 386). Frequently, people vomited during the meal so that they could continue eating (Wolf-Graaf 1983, p. 84). In 1655, an average meal set for the town council consisted of 5 calves, 8 geese, 8 young capons, 6 old chickens, 27 young chickens, 4 suckling pigs, 4 larks and fieldfare, a level measure of lard, 4 pounds of butter, 150 eggs, lemons and other citrus fruits, capers, 2 pounds of bacon, spices, gherkins and about 80 gallons of wine (*Schriftenreihe des mittelalterlichen Kriminalmuseums* 1984, p. 404).

In the Middle Ages, people became intoxicated on beer and wine. This was especially the case on the numerous public holidays and religious festivals. In 1660, there were still 103 public holidays in Paris: Church festivals, weddings, christenings, funerals, Blue Mondays (a Blue Monday was a day off when people had worked the previous Saturday) and other occasions. On working days, beer and wine were consumed as part of the meal. Apart from bread, beer and beer soups formed part of the daily diet of most Europeans.

Drinking contests ad nauseam were a common characteristic of mediaeval life.

This excessive consumption of alcohol during the Middle Ages went hand in hand with the excessive use of spices. Food all but lost its flavour because of the many spices used. The most important ones were salt and pepper, which were also regarded as preservatives. The nobler a household, the more excessive was its consumption of spices. The stronger the pepper burned the mucous membranes of a person who had been invited to a banquet, the greater was his or her respect for the host. Often pepper was used as a substitute for gold to pay for goods. Trade with distant countries boomed as a result of the enormous demand for spices. The great expeditions, the discovery of the New World, the beginning of the Modern Age – all these elements are closely linked to the European demand for pepper (Schivelbusch 1980, pp. 13–24)

Eventually, in the seventeenth and eighteenth centuries, numerous regulations were established to stop boozing and gluttony. Drinking was then allowed only at certain times. The amount of food people were allowed to consume during a wedding or similar events depended on their respective social class (*Schriftenreihe des mittelalterlichen Kriminalmuseums* 1984, pp. 400–9).

In the seventeenth century, a new range of luxury goods came to Europe, including tea, chocolate, sugar and, above all, coffee. Coffee became the established drink of the bourgeoisie. People drank it to sober up and it was believed to have a beneficial effect on the ability to think in abstract terms. The coffee drinker's common sense and business acumen was contrasted with the alcohol drinker's intoxication, incompetence and idleness (Schivelbusch 1980, p. 25).

Chocolate did not have any stimulating effects and was regarded as the counterpart of coffee. It was consumed particularly in Catholic countries since, during the frequent days of fasting, the consumption of beverages was permitted and chocolate represented an important food because of its high nutritional value (Schivelbusch 1980, pp. 96–107).

In the middle of the seventeenth century, tobacco was introduced in France and smoking came into fashion. Smoking had a soothing effect. Due to an increasingly sedentary lifestyle, superfluous energy could be used up by smoking. Smoking represented a very good supplement to coffee for the stimulation of the mind (Schivelbusch 1980, pp. 108–41).

Greater constraints on lifestyle and greater discipline at work were the basis for changes in the consumption of semi-luxury foods and tobacco and direct oral gratification. Legal statutes alone would not have had much effect. One had to find an attractive substitute in order to satisfy these new needs. Coffee and tobacco in particular met these requirements (Schivelbusch 1980, pp. 41–5).

In the sixteenth century, tremendous changes in the area of sexuality can also be observed. In the Middle Ages, sexuality had not yet been reserved for the sanctity of a legitimate marriage. It was quite normal for several people to sleep in one room, among them master and labourers, men and women. Guests often stayed overnight. Usually, everybody slept naked. People who kept on their day-clothes aroused the suspicion that they might be disfigured. It was not before the sixteenth century that special night-clothes were introduced. The bathing customs in the Middle Ages also indicated that people were less inhibited about showing their naked bodies. Knights were served by women when bathing. In the cities, people often took off their clothes at home before walking naked through the city to the public baths (Elias 1978, pp. 163–9).

It was quite common to send a newly wed couple to bed in the presence of witnesses and to watch them consummate the marriage. In the sixteenth century, too, legitimate and illegitimate children were raised together even in the most respectable bourgeois families. The difference was not kept secret from the children, but the legal position of the illegitimate children was generally inferior to that of the legitimate children. Men did not have to be ashamed of their extramarital relationships (Elias 1978, pp. 177–86).

It would be wrong, however, to assume that permissiveness in sexual matters meant greater personal freedom. Although sexual suppression only occurred very late, it had a massive impact and was always accompanied by the menace of bodily harm. Adulterers were often castrated when caught red-handed (Priskil 1983, p. 41). In many cases, lovers and adulterous wives were killed, for example immured or buried alive together (Shahar 1983, pp. 112–15). Generally speaking, castration and the threat of being castrated played an important role in the Middle Ages. Mutilation of parts of the body was a common feature of daily life. For example, if a man made a blasphemous remark, his tongue was torn out. The common punishment for petty thievery was to chop off the thief's fingers or his right hand, while, in case of burglary and theft, the left foot of the culprit was chopped off. In the case of homosexuality, sodomy and sexual intercourse between a Jewish man and a Christian woman, castration was a common means of punishment (Priskil 1983, pp. 41–2).

As long as aggression and sexuality remained within socially accepted limits, few constraints were placed on them. In the Middle Ages, one took great pleasure in fighting, hunting, stealing and killing.

Torture and murder were demonstrated in public and people took great pleasure in watching. Knights were prepared for fighting from a very early age. When firearms were invented in the sixteenth century, different ways of showing aggression developed. On the one hand, the importance of the lower classes grew due to the changes in warfare, and the noblemen on horseback lost a great deal of their influence. Due to these factors the central power of the state increased. On the other hand, killing became more and more anonymous.

Being a clean person in the Middle Ages simply meant wearing neat clothes. The concept of the body as a whole, however, did not yet exist. Only the hands and face had to be clean, as they were the visible parts of the body. This attitude changed in the sixteenth century: the need to change one's underclothes became a 'law of cleanliness'. Even though the cleansing of the skin was not yet envisaged, cleanliness was no longer restricted to the visible parts. Instead, it was applied to the hidden parts of the body, which meant, for example, that a sweat-stained shirt had to be replaced with a clean one. In the sixteenth century, the expenditures for underwear increased rapidly. Those who could afford it had underwear in abundance (Vigarello 1988, pp. 53–111).

This concern for personal hygiene was reinforced by the fear of epidemics like syphilis and the plague. Although humankind had seen serious illnesses since time immemorial, it was the development of cities with increasing numbers of inhabitants and flourishing trade that made it easier for such destructive elements as the plague to spread (Attali 1981, p. 71). In 1347, the plague started in Messina. Massive outbreaks of the disease occurred again and again until the end of the seventeenth century (Tuchmann 1982, p. 97). In the sixteenth century, however, the first specific measures against the plague were taken, such as the closure of public baths (Vigarello 1988, pp. 16–26). Syphilis, as well, which broke out in Naples in 1494 for the first time, spread throughout Europe in the sixteenth century, causing great concern and the fear of contagion (McNeill 1979, p. 202).

In the Early Modern Age, a kind of invisible wall emerged between the individual's body and those of others. Relationships were more reserved. The pressure that people exerted on each other became stronger, demand for good behaviour more insistent and the problem of how to behave properly became more and more important. Trade and finance, job-sharing and co-operation with strangers made it essential to increasingly control desires and to defer emotions. Differentiation within the trades and crafts was the reason for the great increase in professional groups. Everyone exercised a specific trade, and hence became more dependent on others. The transition from external to internal pressure was noticeable. It was only the changes in people's drives and affects, the increasing control of the body and emotions that finally enabled the individual to create the necessary distance from the environment and to acquire the basis of a modern scientific understanding of nature. This encouraged the rapid development of thought in the Early Modern Age (Elias 1976, pp. lx–lxi).

Psychoanalytically speaking, this was the development of the ego taking place, since perception and reality-testing are functions of the ego. According to Jacobson (1973, pp. 123, 132), the ego, which is not capable of reality-testing, is characterised by belief in magic, passiveness, dependence and a lack of autonomy with regard to delegating power to external authorities. In the sixteenth and seventeenth centuries, dramatic changes occurred in people's psychic structure, in their emotions and thought processes, probably as a result of their new living and working conditions. New ways of thinking emerged while the ego became more autonomous and capable of neutralising drives.

A change in the superego began at the same time with changes in control over drives and affects. During the Reformation and also in the course of the Counter-Reformation, the development of an individual conscience and a depersonalised relationship to God began. God was no longer a person beyond time and space, but the voice inside the individual.

" Luther no longer regarded God as someone lurking on the edge of space and time but as him 'who worketh in us' ... One could develop a more personal relationship with this God, who now no longer was just some distant being. (Erikson 1975, p. 235)

If we look at the development of the superego under the aspect of early childhood imagines, we can also observe significant change. Prior to the Reformation, we can see a superego structure in which all parts of the superego were projected. The witch, who embodied the image of the punishing, bad mother, is a forerunner of the oedipal superego. People feared the witch's revenge because of their own immoral behaviour. The Virgin Mary had the function of a forerunner of an ego ideal. Since the good features of the self were projected on to the idealised image of the good mother (Mary), she became the forerunner of the ego-ideal (Klein 1972, p. 109) and satisfied people's infantile desire to become one with their mother (Jacobson 1973, p. 50). The ego was impoverished by this projection and became excessively dependent on the external representatives of its self (Klein 1972, p. 109). Excessive dependence on the Church and other authorities characterises the believer of pre-Reformation times. The demands of the good mother, however, have to be met unconditionally – not only because they represent a part of the self, but also because of earlier fears concerning the good mother. The good mother can quickly turn into an evil one and vice versa (Klein 1972, p. 52; Jacobson 1973, p. 110).

It was not possible to feel depression, guilt and concern of the superego (Kernberg 1967, pp. 672–5). The reactions of the spectators to the execution of the Pappenheimer family, as described in the introduction, show this all too clearly. Executions were like fairs; school classes were taken there for educational purposes (deMause 1974, p. 14) and whole processions made their way to the execution. Punishments, castrations and other cruelties were also carried out publicly. Those who suffered torture did not evoke any concern either. Once the judge of excommunication had declared that the execution of the Pappenheimer family was legitimate, everybody was satisfied and went home. The individual conscience was replaced by the symbols of authority.

In the Early Modern Age, we can see the first signs of a new development of the superego which had become more autonomous. Jacobson (1973, p. 105) describes this as liberation from the pressure of the early, sadistic forerunners of the superego; that of threatening, bad images. If the historic forerunners of the superego are really comparable with the forerunners of the superego in our individual development of today, I will discuss later (Chapter 7). A precondition for this psychic development is the increasing integrating function of the ego, that is, the tremendous ego-development process which had already become evident in the Early Modern Age. This psychic process could not take place without inner conflicts.

5   The Psychic Conflict

The Reformer

At the age of 21, Martin Luther joined the *Schwarzes Kloster*, the Augustinian monastery in Erfurt, thereby fulfilling a vow he had once taken, terrified and horror-stricken, during a thunderstorm. Soon after the completion of his Master's degree *summa cum laude*, he had left the University of Erfurt abruptly and without his father's consent. His father, a miner, had spared no sacrifice to enable his son to study law. Luther's decision to join the monastery therefore met with his father's utter disapproval. Martin Luther was torn between his duty to his father and his obedience to God, whom he believed had called out to him during the thunderstorm (Erikson 1975, pp. 41–3).

At the peak of his career, Luther questioned the obligation to obey God, the Pope, the Emperor, and a great number of other people who demanded obedience in those times. However, Luther was unable to emancipate himself completely from his father's control, which led him to search his soul on the question of the conscience of the individual. Finally, he found a new approach to God which freed him from unconditional obedience to secular and clerical powers. For Luther, an individual's relationship with God became more important.

Throughout his life, Luther was haunted by doubts as to whether he was not merely deceived by the Devil in his efforts. The day the young priest, Martin Luther, read mass for the first time, his father expressed his suspicion that, in reality, the thunderstorm had been the voice of a demon. Possibly his whole career had been motivated by the Devil alone; perhaps indeed it was the Devil who had been responsible for the thunderstorm that had induced Luther to join the monastery and thereby disobey his father? He was haunted by these doubts to such an extent that he often struggled with the Devil all night long, waking up drenched in cold sweat – the Devil's bath, as he called it. (Erikson 1975, pp. 162, 268)

Luther's fear of being possessed became apparent during his infamous fit in the choir, during which he was subjected to frenzy and hysterical laughter, and, startled by his own behaviour, he called out repeatedly: 'No I'm not!' Presumably, he was saying that he was not possessed (Erikson 1975, p. 24). During these struggles, Luther felt that the radiant image of Christ was a mere delusion created by the Devil. He feared Christ and, full of hate, saw in him one who seeks only to punish. He fell unconscious several times, had crying fits, and was subjected to severe states of anxiety. On many of these occasions, he was convinced that his death was near. He completely lost his self-esteem and considered himself to be a 'a pathetic, suffering worm, tormented by the spirit of misery ' (Erikson 1975, p. 269). He suffered from heart problems and poor digestion, constipation and kidney stones and, very much to his annoyance, a buzzing sound in his ears.

Luther was almost torn apart by his throes with the Devil, and, to him, God seemed unforgiving and punishing. If he was indeed afraid of the wrath of God as a consequence of his disobedience, his fear of witches is not surprising. Luther did believe in witches and explicitly favoured their burning at the stake:

" these true harlots of the devil who steal milk, raise storms, ride on goats and brooms and clokes, who shoot, hough or dry out people, who afflict the sucklings in their cradles, who bewitch the marital member and who do more such things ... One should not have mercy upon witches and sorceresses, I would even burn them myself. (Hammes 1977, p. 156)

" That sorceresses should be killed is a most justified law, as they inflict much harm, a fact sometimes ignored. They know how to steal milk, butter and such things from a house by milking a piece of cloth, a table or a handle while pronouncing magic words and thinking of a cow. The Devil will then bring milk and butter to the device employed. Sorceresses can put a spell on children so that they cry bitterly and neither eat nor sleep, etc. They also know how to induce mysterious diseases in a person's knee which exhausts the body. When you see such women, you will recognise them by their devilish looks, I have seen some of them. They must be killed for this reason. (Haustein 1990, p. 123)

However, according to Luther, witches should not be burned because they stole milk, but because they supported the Devil, his sacraments and his church (Haustein 1990, p. 127).

In addition to fearing evil witches and the Devil, Luther lost the protection of the Virgin Mary, although he still turned to St Anne, the patron of miners and therefore of his father, during the thunderstorm that made him take the vow. At the very moment when he was in fear of dying, he needed a motherly mediator, but he decided against the secure path to peace of soul. He took the Virgin Mary down from her pedestal. In an almost scornful way, he would speak of her as one of the female saints who could make a man clasp his arms around her neck or cling to her apron strings.

" As we could never show enough repentance and perform enough good deeds, stark fear and terror would nevertheless remain in the face of His wrath, they told us to call upon the saints in Heaven so that they would speak to Christ in our favour, to call on the Virgin Mary and remind her of the breasts she offered her son so that she pacifies His wrath and obtains His mercy for us. (Erikson 1975, p. 76)

Luther wanted to find a direct path to God, without a mediator. He wanted 'to speak directly, to speak himself, to speak unmolested with his God' (Erikson 1975, p. 105). He appeased God by no longer subjugating himself to Mary and he began to use the Devil to turn his aggression outward towards the worldly rulers. Luther gained autonomy as he overcame splitting and idealisation. God and the Devil became more reconcilable and therefore could be integrated into his personality. He declared the Devil to be the executioner of his martyrdom. Therefore, Luther dominated the Devil and not vice versa. With the help of the Devil, he was able to curse the Pope.

" I cannot pray because I cannot pray without cursing. If I should say hallowed be thy name, I can't help saying damned be the names of all papists and of all those who abuse thy name. When I should say thy kingdom come, I cannot help saying damned and destroyed be the papistry ... verily this is how I pray every day with my mouth and my heart without desisting. (Erikson 1975, p. 272)

In later years, Luther described the Devil, with whom he argued and fought, and whom he sometimes was able to send away, as the other side of life. When something bothered him, it was satisfying for him to realise that the Devil was at work, and he was able to calm himself by uttering an expression of contempt. If, during a wedding ceremony, the wedding ring fell to the floor, he would command the Devil aloud not to interfere (Erikson 1975, p. 274).

For Luther, the two *regna* were able to be integrated, that is, the sphere of divine grace and the sphere of nature, the animalistic nature which exists in the form of inner conflicts within human beings (Erikson 1975, p. 236). As Luther was able to accept the animalistic side of man, he was able to reconcile himself to God without subjugation.

The Possessed

In the Early Modern Age, the phenomenon of possession spread like an epidemic in some regions, and was particularily predominant among women (Schumacher 1937, p.10). Normally, the possessed women were not called witches, but they very often shifted blame for possession onto others and accused them of having used their witchcraft on them. As a consequence, the accused were quite frequently charged with witchcraft and subsequently condemned.

> It is common for possessed people to designate others who were not possessed, as witches. However, it is incomparably less common for the possessed themselves to be suspected of being witches. (Ernst 1972, p. 25)

It seems that there existed a certain form of psychopathology during the centuries of the witch persecutions: The young woman who had acute psychic problems, showing signs of spasms, St Vitus' dance, seizures, an altered voice and gestures, was considered possessed and an attempt was made to help her. The old woman who was chronically distrustful, who had an inclination to let fly with a stream of abuse and who vegetated away in her shabby hut was soon suspected of being a witch, was tortured and executed (Ernst 1972, p. 124).

The possessed were convinced that their true soul had been fettered and oppressed by a demon who had entered and possessed it. It was not they who would performed certain actions, but the Devil. Nicole le Roy, for instance, believed that whenever she crossed herself with her right hand and then hit it with her left hand involuntarily, the Devil had made her hand do so (Ernst 1972, pp. 56–9). The state of possession was frequenty characterised by symptoms like states of agitation, convulsions, spasms, swallowing of air, stiffness, paralysis, insensitivity to pain, deafness, muteness, blindness, puerilism and signs of an alternating personality, as described in the above-mentioned case of Nicole le Roy. Occasionally, the possessed also excreted foreign bodies such as pins or nails or possessed such extraordinary strength that six strong men were not able to subdue her. Quite frequently, the possessed reported that the Devil led them to certain places.

An 'office of exorcism' originated in the third century. It was part of the exorcism ritual to ask the demon's name. The Devil was forced by threats to leave the body of the possessed, and he gave a sign when he had done so. Exorcism was supposed to take place in a church, where the possessed was expected to pray, confess and take communion.

Usually it took several hours for the entire ritual to be carried out (Ernst 1972, pp. 18–19).

Let us examine a few cases of possession in the Early Modern Age more closely. Nicole Obri (Ernst 1972, pp. 32–51) was born the daughter of a butcher in the village of Vervins, some 40 km from the bishopric of Laon. At the age of 15, when she had been married for barely three months, the first symptoms of possession manifested themselves. Her family had a regular income, and Nicole herself, who is said to have been very pretty, had spent several years in a convent where, despite this, she had gained only a poor mastery of reading. In November 1565, Nicole prayed by the grave of her grandfather who had died unexpectedly without having confessed. Suddenly she became aware of a man who was wrapped in a shroud. After seeing this apparition, she was bereft of sleep, refused to eat, and longed to return to her parents; they, however, sent her back to her husband. A few days later, the man in the shroud appeared anew and demanded that she send her husband on pilgrimages for her grandfather's redemption. However, when bad weather kept Nicole's husband from undertaking some of the required pilgrimages, her condition deteriorated. Before long she had become extremely agitated, she banged her head against the wall of the house, tried to throw herself into the fire, and soon afterwards went deaf, dumb, blind and her whole body became stiff. Following each occurrence, she was unable to recall what she had done.

What had begun as an apparition of a man wrapped in a shroud ended with Nicole being possessed by the Devil. The Devil abducted her and took her away to a pigsty, or she was found talking to an invisible person. Once she was officially deemed possessed, the community rallied behind her. Public prayers and processions were ordered. Every day, six men carried Nicole, thrashing about and screaming, to the church of Vernins. The Devil's rage grew stronger, Nicole's face turned dark blue, her body seemed to swell and her screams could be heard across the marketplace. In church the Devil never left her in peace and Nicole only calmed down when she was taken back to her parents' house.

During a private exorcism, where only relatives were present, the Devil was asked why he had possessed Nicole. He told them that Nicole's mother had cursed her four years before, that is, the girl had been given to the Devil when she had gone dancing instead of looking after her little sister. On this occasion the little girl had lost her rosary. When Nicole returned home, her mother wanted to beat her. It was with her mother's curse that the change in Nicole's state of mind began. At the riverside, the Devil made her stumble in order to drown her. And it was at the Devil's instigation that Nicole tried to steal her grandfather's money so she could run away, but she could not open the money box. She stole towels, bed linen and dishes and sold the stolen goods to a receiver. The Devil made her fall down the cellar stairs. Several times she was publicly exorcised in Laon and every time a huge crowd flocked into the cathedral to see how the Devil left Nicole's body when a host was put in her mouth. Afterwards, she was a different person. The Devil always fought against the exorcism. For example, everyone in the coach was suddenly stricken with a severe headache on their way to the cathedral. By then Nicole was possessed by 30 demons and was publicly exorcised in various pilgrimage churches and in the diocesan town. There, she uttered blasphemies, arched her body and balanced on her head and feet so that, to the great dismay of those present, her private parts could be seen. She only calmed down when a host was placed on her. This was regarded as proof that the host is the body of Christ, thus contradicting the Huguenot claim.

It is likely that the symptoms never completely disappeared. In 1577 it was reported that she had recovered from blindness that had lasted for several months. She was imprisoned twice and was in danger of being executed. The enormous commitment to the possessed is characteristic of that time, even though this could change if the trials took an unpredictable turn. Unlike many other possessed people, Nicole did not accuse anyone of having bewitched her. Her inhibitions about accusing her own parents were probably too strong. However, Nicole's immoral conduct and her mother's fateful curse clearly demonstrates Nicole's inner conflict. Being cursed by one's parents was a classic motive for becoming possessed (Ernst 1972, p. 37).

Nicole feared the punishment (the curse) for her aggressive conduct and her longing for autonomy and sexual activity (dancing). By splitting and projecting her own impulses on to the Devil, she tried to defend them. At the same time, the Devil took over the function of self-punishment (turning aggression against the self). He caused Nicole to fall down the cellar stairs. The inner defence was strengthened by the submission to the ecclesiastical authorities and to the incorporation of the body of Christ. Through her ascetic behaviour (Nicole sent her husband on dangerous pilgrimages), she tried to repress her own sexual desires which she experienced as immoral. The conflict of the superego (fear of persecution caused by the curse) is defended by splitting, projection and primitive idealisation (the body of Christ). Nicole thereby loses some of her autonomy by being submitted either to the Church or to split impulses.

The well-documented story of Anna Göldin (Hasler 1982) describes the relationship between Anna Maria Tschudi, who became possessed when she was nine, and the maidservant Anna Göldin who was the last woman executed as a witch in Switzerland. Anna Göldin was born in Glarus in 1734. When Anna was 14, her mother sent her away from home after a farm labourer had tried to assault her. Her father was already dead. She worked as a maidservant in different households, was twice pregnant but lost both children at birth. Anna Göldin was charged with infanticide and punished. In 1780 she took up work in the household of a physician named Tschudi. The Tschudis had two daughters, Susanna and Anna Maria, and a son named Heinrich. Susanna was considered to be more clever than her sister. Anna Maria soon began to seek the maidservant's friendship, accompanied her on her errands and slept in her bed at night because she was frightened. Mrs Tschudi did not like Anna too much. She thought the girl vain and felt that she made the children cling to her. She also became aware of her husband's advances towards the maidservant. At the end of a year's time, an argument with serious consequences took place. In the kitchen, Anna Maria pushed the maidservant's bonnet off her head, and Anna Göldin responded by giving her a shove. The mother, who did not know the facts, punished her daughter Susanna. Anna Göldin explained that she had punished the wrong daughter. A few days later, the first pin was found in Anna Maria's milk; the girl was then nine years old. From then on, pins were found in her milk every day. Anna Maria blamed the maidservant, and Anna Göldin was dismissed.

Anna Maria suffered from severe convulsions; she writhed in contortions on the floor, and she spat out pins and pieces of iron wire. In addition to this, her left leg became paralysed. She only had fits during the daytime and everybody in the village pitied her. Every day visitors came, sat down at her bedside and observed the child. The bed was covered with bed linen made of the finest Belgian lace.

The maid went to live with her cousin and eventually her sister. All the money she had saved in 25 years, 16 Swiss Doubloons, was seized and kept by the local authorities. Rumours spread that the head of the household made Anna Göldin pregnant. Only after these accusations did they search for and arrest the maid. She vehemently denied having bewitched Anna Maria, but was forced to take a look at the girl and her awful condition. When the maid was brought to the child, she prayed for her and moved her legs, whereupon the child's condition promptly improved. The maid was tortured, confessed, and in 1782 became the last witch to be executed in Switzerland.

The story of Anna Göldin demonstrates the relation between a possessed person and the person accused of being a witch. Anna Maria loved the maid, and as she was the child loved least by her parents, she sought the maid's affection. When the maid took her sister's side, Anna Maria was probably very disillusioned. Due to her anger, her picture of the good mother was changed into that of a mean witch who punished and persecuted her. In the girl's mind, the beloved maid changed into a mean witch. The good milk turned into destructive milk with pins. This can be compared to the accusations of witchcraft against people who were not possessed, insofar as it also displays immoral behaviour on the part of the accuser whose aggressions and fear of persecution were probably increased by the disillusionment in the maid. The inner conflict was overcome by accusing the maid as a means of projective identification. As was the case with Nicole, the Devil acts out the impulse (immoral behaviour) as well as the defence mechanism, which is the unconscious, auto-aggressive self-punishment manifested in the eating of pins.

The splitting into opposite states of consciousness (dissociation) was largely due to a wish to defend aggressions. By turning the aggressions toward the outside by accusing someone of being a witch, and the subsequent execution of the accused person, aggressions could be mastered. This is why a successful accusation improved the condition of the possessed.

In the Early Modern Age, virtual epidemics of possessions broke out quite often in convents (Ernst 1972, p. 97). The case of the nuns Madelaine de Demandouls and Louise Capeau, was widely known (Ernst 1972, pp. 98–108; Michelet 1974, pp. 144–58). Madelaine became ill from possession at her convent in Aix when she was 19. She was brought to St Baume to be exorcised, when Louise, another nun, started to show signs of possession as well. Louise became possessed only after she saw how much attention Madelaine was receiving from other people. Both nuns showed hostility towards each other. Louise delivered sermons in the name of the Devil and Madelaine tried to interrupt her by shouting and screaming. Louise humiliated and insulted Madelaine, whereas Madelaine's states of excitement were less vehement. In the name of her Devil, Louise maintained that Madelaine had been seduced on a witches' sabbath by the young priest, Gauffridy.

Madelaine herself stated that she had been seduced by Gauffridy and had been bewitched by him after she had entered the convent (Ernst 1972, p. 100). Michelet confirms that Gauffridy had seduced his pupil, but did not want to marry her, which drove her to enter the convent out of fear and shame (Michelet 1974, p. 143). Madelaine's states of excitement became more pronounced; she writhed around on the floor in an obscene way and declared she had been the queen of a witches' sabbath in St Baume where the king had been Gauffridy who had seduced her there. Gauffridy was commanded to appear in St Baume. As he could not defend himself against the accusations of the two women, he was tortured. Following severe torture, he confessed, and was burned to death in 1611. Following his execution, Madelaine's symptoms disappeared, and she began to go around with poor women gathering wood, which she sold for a pittance. Louise revealed other names of individuals suspected of sorcery, including a poor, blind girl who was also burned (Ernst 1972, pp. 105–6).

Again and again, nuns accused priests – and sometimes other nuns – of having caused their possessed state. Conflicts due to life in a convent, sexual fantasies, desires and disappointments were resolved through accusations of witchcraft. An epidemic evolved from a case of possession, when another nun became jealous of the attention received by a possessed nun. Possession epidemics occurred in Auxonne between 1658 and 1663 (Ernst 1972, p. 113), and in Loudun between 1632 and 1634 (Michelet 1974, pp. 158–69).

The situation that usually led up to a possession often involved disappointments and failures, for example: a mother's curse (Nicole Obri), betrayal of the beloved maid-servant (Anna Tschudi), the unrequited love of a priest (Madelaine de Demandouls) or the attention heaped on a fellow nun (Louise Capeau). Leading up to the disappointment was also the immoral behavior of the possessed person. Nicole did not take care of her little sister; Anna knocked the bonnet off of the maid's head, and Madelaine gave herself to the priest.

People who were considered possessed tried to cope with their sexual and aggressive impulses by developing a split self (dissociation) following disappointments and rejection. This led to fear of persecution (archaic feeling of guilt). The person possessed suffered from an inner psychic conflict resulting in splitting, projection on to the Devil and submission to contrary ascetic ideals which triggered the symptoms of possession. During the process of the projective identification, this affect could be externalised and thus lead to the relief of the symptoms by accusing a person of witchcraft. This splitting apparently enhanced the ego-defence through an idealisation of the external object which had already existed before the state of possession occurred – as was the case with the maid Anna – in order to defend earlier disappointments and deprivations. The exorcisms resulted in extensive public attention for the possessed (secondary gain). This attention, along with praying for support from the Virgin Mary (the idealised 'good mother') and through the help of asexual confessors, helped to suppress the oppressed impulses, thus alleviating the symptoms. The disappointment experienced in the trigger situation was followed by regression and led to an excessive splitting (dissociation). According to Klein (1972, pp. 122–3; pp. 149–50), the individual self is not able to work through the integration of good and bad images as long as the fear of persecution and the processes of splitting are too strong. Regression and the fear of persecution, as well as the splitting, are enforced in such a way that part of the self is split off from the rest. But why were women in particular possessed?

Girls certainly had to cope with rejection and disappointment more often than boys and, above all, they had to deal with a higher degree of oppression of the drives. Thus, even a minor incident could trigger regression and the symptoms of possession. Moreover, during their upbringing, girls learned to turn aggressive impulses against themselves more than boys.

Historical evidence shows that girls have always been more often the victims of child murder than boys (Piers 1976, p. 421). The reduced status of girls is also evident in the fact that in seventeenth-century France, there were derogatory or scatological names commonly used for girls (Marvick 1974, p. 284). Letters of that time reveal the general negative attitude towards girls:

> The father is such a good and wise and reasonable man that he is fond of girls as well as of boys. However, it would be a great consolation for you to also have boys so that the memory of your good name won't fade as soon as it will without sons, because, as you well know, girls do not make families but rather 'unmake' them. (Ross 1974, p. 206)

The upper class in particular wanted to have heirs. The steadily increasing dowry was another reason why sons were preferred to daughters. It was common belief that by merely looking at a pregnant woman, one was able to tell whether she was going to give birth to a boy or a girl:

> A woman whose color was good and body temperature comfortably warm might expect a boy, while if she were carrying a girl she would be distinguished by 'a pale, heavy, and swarth countenance, a melancolique eye: she is wayward, fretful, and sad... her face is spotted with red ...'. (Illick 1974, p. 304)

Mothers usually breast-fed male babies for about two years, while female babies were only breast-fed for one year (McLaughlin 1974, p. 116).

The case of Anna Tschudi suggests that these preconditions for socialisation, which clearly put women at a disadvantage, had a considerable effect on women's psychic development in Early Modern times and therefore affected the preconditions for possession as well. Anna Tschudi was an unloved child; her parents preferred her sister who was considered to be more intelligent (Hasler 1982, pp. 42–3). To cope with her aggressions and to ward off the image of the all bad mother, she idealised the maid (the image of an all good mother). The fact that the maid protected her sister proved to be very frustrating for Anna, and as a consequence, the symptoms of the possession began to occur. The image of the all bad mother, that is, the witch, was projected on to the maid.

The Changeling

One of the less well known phenomena of the witch persecutions is the changeling. Sickly, deformed children or those with strong behavioural disorders were said to be the offspring of the Devil and a witch.

Throughout human history, physical discomfort of the expectant mother and illnesses of the young child have been attributed to the influence of evil beings. A child had to be protected from a large number of hostile powers: blood- and marrow-sucking vampires, spirits that caused illnesses and child-stealing demons. Malevolent spirits tried to rob or exchange the helpless infant because, as German folklore tells us, they longed for beautiful human children to improve their own race. Deformed children whose physical peculiarities could not be explained satisfactorily have always been subjected to special consideration (Appel 1937, pp. 5–14).

The typical changeling was generally described as small and ugly, with a large head and small hands. Sometimes it was pot-bellied and had very thin legs. On average, these small, deformed creatures died by the age of twelve. According to folklore, they were so voracious that not even four or five women had enough milk to feed it. These symptoms indicate diseases that are known in contemporary science as cretinism, hydrocephalus or rickets.

The origin of the word 'changeling' dates back to mediaeval times when changelings were believed to be children exchanged for human children by demons. This exchange process, however, could be prevented with the help of protective magic. For instance, parents were advised to keep a candle burning beside the cradle until the infant was baptised, to put an object made of steel into the cradle, leave the cradle on the floor boards, and so on. It was also believed that one's own children would be returned if the changeling was ignored by the mother, beaten or left hungry and crying. Once the changeling was touched, it would remain with the family. The cooking of eggshells or shoe-soles, for example, would make the changeling talk or laugh. This would reveal the changeling's true nature and it would consequently be taken back by the demons. Pagan demons – not the Devil – were after the little children. In the original concepts of a changeling, it was always asserted that the mother was entirely innocent in having given birth to such a creature. Instead, demons were blamed for the child's deformations.

> To one mother it happened that elves took her child out of the cradle and put in a changeling instead with a huge head and rigid eyes, who refused to eat and drink. In her misery she went to the woman next door and asked her advice. The latter told her to carry the changeling to the kitchen, put him on top of the stove, light a fire and boil water in two eggshells; this would make the changeling laugh, and if he laughed that would expose him as a changeling. The woman followed her advice, and as she put the eggshells with water on to boil, the changeling said, 'Now I've become as old as the Westerwald and have never seen anyone boiling water in shells!', and started laughing, and as he laughed, suddenly a number of elves brought in the right child, put it on top of the stove and took away their companion. (Appel 1937, p. 6)

The typical structure of the legend was the theft of the beautiful human child and the recognition of the changeling's true nature, the use of protective magic and the return of the human child. Sometimes it was also assumed that the demons treated the human child in the same way as the changeling was treated by the family.

Thus, misshapen or handicapped children were not always killed. Blaming external forces made tolerant behaviour toward deformation possible. The mothers had given birth to beautiful children who were then exchanged by demons. The child's handicap was not a narcissistic insult to the mother; she had given birth to a beautiful child who was taken from her. Touching the child, talking to it or laughing with it might have changed the mother's perception of the child and made her accept it as her own. Touching, talking and laughing were expressions of the bond between mother and child. If the mother's child was treated well by the demons, it was only rational for her to treat the handicapped child in the same way. In the fourteenth century a certain tolerance towards handicapped people could still be observed. They were free to move about in society, as long as they did not pose a threat to other people.

> Persons who suffered from minor mental handicaps were not usually locked up, but were allowed to move freely among their neighbours, as could the crippled, the spastics, the scrofulous and other misfits. (Tuchman 1982, p. 465)

Until the late Middle Ages, many children from higher social classes who were born with a handicap were taken to monasteries or convents.

" This (i.e. the handing over of children to the monastery) was done to ensure their care in keeping with their social status, especially if they were in some way physically impaired. Names of famous writers of the late Middle Ages such as Hermann the Lame (contractus) and Notker the Stutterer (labeo) illustrate this fact. (Arnold 1980, p. 22)

When the belief in witches and the Devil eventually began to predominate in the sixteenth and seventeenth centuries, the attitude towards disabled and handicapped people changed. Although the children were still called 'changelings', they were no longer considered to have been exchanged by demons, but to be the fruit of a sexual relationship between the Devil and a witch. A congenital disability or handicap raised the question as to its cause, this at a time when all sexual impulses were suppressed, and so was connected with forbidden sexuality.

Deformed people and cripples who had supposedly been fathered by the Devil (Hammes 1977, p. 84) were exhibited at fairs. Since the deformed children were the result of contact with the Devil, no one cared if they perished (Graf 1936, p.196). For disabled persons, the consequences arising from the obsessive belief in witches became apparent when in Osnabrück, Germany, 160 mentally handicapped persons were burnt at the stake as witches and warlocks. Luther was also of the opinion that the changelings were only a mass of soulless flesh and he advised drowning them (Meyer 1983, p.91). This change in perspective was expressed in *The Witch Hammer*:

" For some are always ailing and crying, and yet the milk of four women is not enough to satisfy them. Some are generated by the operation of Incubus devils, of whom, however, they are not the sons, but of that man from whom the devil has received the semen as a Succubus, or whose semen he has collected from some nocturnal pollution in sleep. For these children are sometimes, by Divine permission, substituted for the real children.

" And there is a third kind, when the devils at times appear in the form of young children and attach themselves to nurses. But all three kinds have this in common, that though they are very heavy, they are always ailing and do not grow, and cannot receive enough milk to satisfy them, and are often reported to have vanished away. (Sprenger and Institoris 1971, part 2, p. 192)

While the topic of the original legend of the changeling still emerges in the text above, the very question as to why God permits this to happen involves adultery committed by the wife. The deformation was attributed to the woman's forbidden sexuality:

" And if a jealous husband cannot suffer even a hint of adultery, how much more will he be disturbed when adultery is actually committed! Therefore, it is no wonder if their own children are taken away and adulterous children substituted. (Sprenger and Institoris 1971, part 2, p. 192)

Sprenger and Institoris stated that adultery with the Devil had the same quality as real adultery. This statement was understandable if the Devil represented one's own desires. At this point, the sexuality of the mother was now made responsible for the child's handicap.

However, the persecution and extermination of disabled persons apparently never took place on the same scale as witch persecutions in the Early Modern Age. Thomas (1979, p. 296) even doubts that disabled persons were really killed because they were considered children of the Devil. From his point of view, they were just victims of the obsessive belief in witches because, due to their social situation, they were forced to beg and thus fit into the typical pattern of those accused of witchcraft.

Child Witnesses

In numerous witch trials, children denounced other persons as witches. Often, the children accused close relatives: parents, grandparents, cousins or neighbours (Weber 1996, p. 21). Who were these children?

Often, they were poor, deserted and dispossessed. Their behaviour was conspicuous and they were often orphans or half-orphans living in other people's homes or on the streets. The children were regarded as sexually active and sinfully seductive; they had fantasies about sleeping with the Devil. In most cases, they had had real sexual experience. This fact leads Weber (1996, pp. 176–82). to describe them as sexually abused children for whom the accusation of witchcraft was an opportunity to take revenge and express their feelings mythologically. In comparison, Sebald (1996) sees the children who served as witnesses as evidence for the fantasies and untrustworthiness of children. These assessments are reflected in the current discourse on child abuse.

Weber (1996, p. 186) reports that sexual abuse had taken place in about a quarter of the 37 cases he had investigated in Baden-Württemberg, Germany. In half of the cases, sexual seduction was likely. According to Weber, in particular the realistic details of seduction and rape are an indication that sexual abuse had actually taken place. Barbara Schurtz from Weinsberg, Germany, reports a seduction by an adult in 1662:

> She said the devil had grabbed her and carried her through a hole in the hedges, where he laid her body naked to the waist. Suddenly he appeared to her not as the devil anymore, but as a man. The man, she said, was red all over his belly and his whole body. On the belly, she added, he also had hair. (Weber 1996, pp. 179–80)

In this case, the girl was examined by three midwives who stated that the girl must have been raped not only once but several times. The girl was taken to a hospital, where she suffered from nightmares in which the Devil visited her.

Most of the children were already disobedient and rebellious before having been seduced by the Devil. After seduction, the children were very afraid that they would have to attend the witch dance, and they could not sleep. With respect to gender, girls and boys were equally affected. While the youngest child was four years old, most of the children were between seven and ten years old (Weber 1996, p.104).

Children often denounced themselves for having slept with the Devil. From the beginning, this self-denunciation had the purpose of implicating someone else (Weber 1996, p. 132). Death penalties for children who after all had denounced themselves in a dangerous way were only rarely pronounced and carried out. Usually, the children were punished in public with a stroke of the cane, or a priest was engaged to pray with and for them. In most cases, didactic and Christian influences were preferred to corporal punishment (Weber 1996, pp. 133–6).

In the year 1628, the Walters, a married couple from Alpirsbach (Germany), took proceedings against the 50-year-old ladykiller, spendthrift and habitual debtor, Lorentz Khünin, who had been married for eight years without having children, for raping their 12-year-old daughter Anna. The child reported that Lorentz Khünin had taken her by the hand and led her into the farm labourer's room. He had laid her on the bed and had wanted to perform an unchaste act with her. She said that there had been five more such incidents.

Anna Walter was baptised in 1615, her father died in 1626, and her mother married Bartlin Walter. Anna and her mother moved to the stepfather's home. Anna was considered a nasty, precocious girl. She was such an odd child that sometimes people thought her to be out of her mind.

Khünin first denied all allegations but finally declared that the girl herself had pursued him. She had instructed him to touch her, but he had not had intercourse with her. He believed that she was still a virgin. Certain respectable women examined the girl. They found that the girl had lost her virginity by force. In the course of the trial, however, the situation completely changed and the girl was then suspected of being a witch because she talked in an impudent, obscene and provocative way to the warden of the monastery. After Anna was accused, she confessed that she had indeed been in contact with an evil spirit. He had come to her as a man in knickerbockers, had promised her presents and had finally caused her downfall. Like a lover, he had taken a lock of her hair and had told her not to pray any longer or wash her hands in the morning. Then the girl admitted that Lorentz Khünin had not been the first man she had slept with. The first had been the blacksmith, Michael Hasenmayer, and the second the shepherd, Jacob. Then she said that she had been sleeping with the Devil for four years and that he had been her first sexual partner. These were very serious self-accusations.

However, since Anna had harmed neither humans nor animals, but had simply fornicated with the Devil, the priest was told to save the child's body and soul and pray for her. She was sent to a hospital, where she kept claiming that the Devil came to sleep with her. Finally she declared that her mother had taught her everything about witchcraft and that her mother had already given her to the Devil when she was still very young. As the court did not proceed against her mother, Anna wished that her mother be beheaded. When the girl showed no improvement after two years in the hospital, she was sent to another one (Weber 1991, pp. 50–6).

Anna clearly shows signs of a girl who had been sexually abused. Her sexually provocative behaviour makes her repeatedly relive the abuse, suffering again and again. Accusing her mother of being a witch gave her the chance to express her aggressions against her mother who was not able to protect her. As in most cases, the girl was lavishly cared for. Astonishingly, in this case, the mother was not put on trial.

Elisabeth Widmar, a nine-year-old girl from Sulz on the Neckar, had stolen a loaf of bread. In 1626 her case was investigated and she was locked up in a madhouse. The girl then started telling stories about a 'black man' who first appeared as a fatherly friend and later as a seducer. Elisabeth's parents had gone to war and had given their children to a nurse. During this time, the children were given only hay to eat instead of bread. Elisabeth tried to survive by stealing cake, cheese, butter, bread and meat. Her father made sure she had a strict Christian upbringing. He sent her to worship and disciplined her severely. He often beat her and even threatened to beat her to death.

Elisabeth's claims about the Devil led to a trial in which she first depicted him as someone who had helped, consoled and saved her and had promised her bread and then – as a white man – seduced her. Again, what she said included realistic details. The man had hurt her. In the shed, the white man had lain down with her and had his way with her. This had hurt the girl terribly, and afterwards she had cried.

Elisabeth attracted attention through her sexual activity. Allegedly, she fornicated with the Devil and lusted after boys. Adolescent boys ran after her and even visited her in prison. Elisabeth now claimed her brother had seduced her into witchcraft. Then again, she accused her brothers and sisters and numerous men and women from the town, among them her cousin Maria Haug.

Her parents denied all responsibility in the incidents. Their daughter had always been wild and unruly, they said. She had never behaved in a way one would expect of a good child. Only when no measures had any effect was she beaten with rods. As Elisabeth continued with her accusations, her father upbraided her, declared her to be a witch and no longer his child. Elisabeth did not want to return to her father or mother and preferred to scrape by as a tramp and beggar.

Meanwhile, her cousin Maria Haug confessed under torture to Elisabeth's accusations. In 1626, she was beheaded and burnt. Elisabeth continued to refuse to pray. One day she tried to strangle herself with her underwear. At the Devil's command, she attempted suicide several times. Yet there was still reluctance to sentence her to death; in the spital she could be cared for and educated in a Christian way and be punished by caning. The priest declared that he would approve of her being sentenced to death. After the execution of her cousin, whom she had accused of being a seductress, she denounced her own mother, saying it had been her mother who had offered her to the Devil and who had given her the Devil's mark. After regaining consciousness following a further suicide attempt, she said that her mother had visited her and had wanted to kill her. The mother had already aroused suspicion of witchcraft several years earlier, before she was married. In addition, Elisabeth denounced the head of the nunnery, who was thereupon taken into custody, lost her position and, in the end, had to pay the costs of the proceedings. In all, 24 people were accused by the girl.

Elizabeth was rebaptised and finally, the Devil stopped pursuing her. By 1628, she was considered healed and planned to attend mass and go to school. The community thanked the Lord that their attempt to rescue the poor girl from the grip of the evil enemy had been successful (Weber 1996, pp. 137–41).

Since the behaviour and the accusations of the child witnesses were signs of neglect and/or sexual abuse, it seems rather striking with what tremendous zeal the people took care of these children and how eagerly they tried to free them from sexuality, that is, the Devil. The idea of a Devil, though, also diverted attention from the accusations against human seducers, mostly male, because the Devil in such cases could be blamed for indecent deeds instead of them. Men escaped charges, while the adult females, the mothers and women who were accused of witchery in these trials, were burnt at the stake. In 1665, the eight-year-old orphan Marcel Lutz, shared a bed with his cousin Margarethe. The circumstances suggested that he had taken the initiative in their erotic encounters. At the same time, he desired another girl, but when he was turned down, he denounced her as a witch. It was probably only thanks to her young age that the girl was spared the death penalty (Weber 1996, pp. 169–70).

If a woman makes a pact with the Devil, she gains control over her sexuality, and self-determined sexuality incited fear in the people of those times, but only if adult females were involved. In the case of younger ones, it was hoped that they could still be 'saved'. During the interrogations of the alleged witches, they were asked whether the Devil had slept with them after the conclusion of the pact, what his penis and his semen had been like, whether coitus with the Devil had been exceptionally satisfying, whether he had had intercourse with her several times during the night in question and whether he had ejaculated. There were also questions about whether the Devil had slept with her in a 'natural' manner, and whether the defendant had been made pregnant by various men (Weber 1996, p. 150).

Acknowledging the Devil gave men the opportunity to project guilt and responsibility on to the women for their own wish to gain power and control in sexual matters, for their feelings of aggression and disappointments as well as for rapes. As the witch represents the oedipal threatening image of the mother, strong unconscious guilt feelings about oedipal strivings and fears could be easily projected on to the women, who became witches. The sexually abused or mistreated children all showed signs of sexualisation, a defence mechanism of the ego (see Chapters 6 and 7). The image of the Devil helped them to master the passively suffered trauma by active and sexualising behaviour.

The Living Saints

In the fourteenth and fifteenth century, there were several spiritual women whose lives fluctuated between saintly veneration and accusations of witchery. Were they saints or were they witches who had formed an evil pact with the Devil? The reputation of being a saint could easily turn suddenly into an accusation of witchery.

Margery Kempe (approximately 1373–1439) lived in England, was married to a tradesman and had 14 children. She was deeply religious and led the life of a pilgrim, which took her to distant places such as Italy, Norway and Germany. At God's command, she was always clad in white to reflect her virginity and her close relationship to Jesus Christ as his bride. This mode of attire was considered highly provocative in those days, as she was no longer a virgin. After she had given birth to her first child, she was tormented and tortured by demons for six months, but the Lord rescued her with his consolation. She saw visions, uttered prophecies and believed in divine betrothal. She also demonstrated the gift of tears. This manifested itself in crying and screaming fits during which she suffered the pain of the Redeemer, and she became so agitated during communion that two men had to hold her.

The charismatic gift of tears, the capacity to weep out of religous devotion, was highly esteemed in the Catholic Church. The severe crying fits, however, repeatedly raised the question of whether they were caused by the Holy Spirit or the Devil in the body. At the pilgrimage church in Canterbury, the monks turned against Margery and wanted to burn her as a heretic. Much the same thing happened in Leicester, where she was supposed to be charged. In York she was thrown into a dungeon, but there she was again taken care of by numerous lay people. The Archbishop felt she was possessed. The reactions were split each time: she had both supporters and bitter enemies (Dinzelbacher 1995, pp. 15–20).

Colomba von Rieti (1467–1503) moved to Perugia (Italy) in 1488 and showed all of the common phenomena of a living saint: ecstatic trances, prophecies, healings and particularly abstinence from food. She confessed and prayed every day in church, where she was adulated almost as if she were the Virgin Mary. When the plague approached the city in 1494, she was asked to intercede. She ordered that processions of penitence be held and she cured hundreds with her mere touch or with oil from her lamp. She became infected herself, but was saved through mystical apparitions. An annual procession was proclaimed in her honour while she was still alive, but she also had many enemies who wanted to have her burned as a heretic. Nevertheless, she withstood all the tests and medical examinations related to her abstinence from food (Dinzelbacher 1995, pp. 28–32).

Eustochio of Padua (1444–1469), was an unwanted and unhappy child, the fruit of adultery between a married man and a nun. She was born in a convent, was given away by her mother and grew up in her father's house with a mean stepmother. Her father was afraid that Eustochio would poison him because he was so strict towards her. He returned her to the convent where she had been born. As a child, she was considered possessed. She told how she was carried through the air by the Devil and was disobedient, but all exorcisms were in vain, just like the brutal punishments meted out by her stepmother.

In the convent Eustochio had convulsions, showed the whites of her eyes, clutched at her hair, gnashed her teeth, and emitted ghastly screams while her face changed colours. She would slither around like a snake only to spring up suddenly into the air. She attacked the other nuns with a knife, threw a stone at the father confessor and then collapsed in a state of paralysis. Her painful convulsions alternated with moments during which she thanked God for the agony visited upon her. The father confessor believed that Eustochio was innocent, and that, although her behaviour was caused by the evil spirit, she repeatedly had periods when she demonstrated exemplary humility and devout behaviour.

When the abbess of the convent took ill, an attempt was made to take a certain Eustochio to court for witchcraft. She was thrown into a dungeon. People mobbed the convent and demanded that Eustochio be burned alive for witchcraft, without a trial. When her father confessor spoke up for her, he was suspected of witchcraft as well. He was permitted to speak with her, and she confessed to being a sorceress, and claimed that the other nuns had instructed her. She later recanted, and the fact that the abbess recovered probably saved her life. Despite everything that had occurred, she was unwilling to leave the convent. She insisted on martyrdom, claiming that her agonies were merely the tokens of love that the heavenly bridegroom sent her, and in following Christ, she had to make her way to heaven on a path of thorns. Her seizures became worse and she appeared to have been beaten black and blue, and bled from cuts and flagellation wounds. She had to swallow water with disgusting ingredients, and she vomited blood. The demon took off her clothes and tried to wring her neck. After she had been permitted to take her vows in 1465, the symptoms seemed to improve, and through the humility she displayed in her suffering, she steadily gained a reputation for sanctity. She died in 1469, weakened by the daily loss of blood, and in the eighteenth century, she was beatified by Pope Clemens XIII (Dinzelbacher 1995, pp. 35–9).

In the seventeenth century, an increasing number of saints who were trying to create a holy aura around themselves, mainly by fasting, were discovered to be frauds. In Augsburg, Anna Laminit (laminit: one who does not eat) was regarded as a living saint in the sixteenth century. She wore a penitential robe at all times and was never clad in anything but black. She experienced revelations from God, saw visions and appearances of angels. At her command, the largest procession ever held in Augsburg took place there in 1503, during which virgins in black hair shirts carried candles. Anna's reputation as a saint was not tarnished by the fact that she had led a rather indecent life in her youth. She had been pilloried for procuration and other abominations, and had been driven out of the city with sticks. She had two sons out of wedlock. The saintliness of this woman was founded on her complete abstention from food. She claimed that she had lived completely without food since 1498, and that she had not even touched the host. She also claimed that she had not defecated in 14 years. However, suspicion began to arise and in 1512, her deception was discovered. While she was staying in the duchess' guest room, someone looked through a hole in the wall and saw her eating. She was banned from the city. She later remarried and, after her husband's death, was charged with various more mundane frauds and was later drowned (Dinzelbacher 1995, pp. 79–82).

This case shows that the reputation of a saint could turn very quickly into that of a witch. The women mentioned above wanted to be saints because of their wish to repulse their inner aggressions and carnal desires. Margery had borne 14 children, yet she wanted to be considered a virgin, while Anna Laminit was in the business of arranging extramarital contacts. As a result of their repulsion of carnal desires, these women were venerated, rather than being burned as witches, they were usually cared for like the possessed. Whenever women gave up their fight against sexuality, which was to be mastered through submission to God, and demanded sexual gratification for themselves, the image of the witch, a reversal into the opposite as defence mechanism, was present. The inability of a woman to weep was a sign that she was a witch, and was contrasted with the divine gift of weeping. Witches desecrate the host, while saints live from it. The pact with the Devil corresponds to a betrothal with Christ. On the one hand, there are visions of Christ; on the other, apparitions of the Devil. The brides of Christ are bound by divine expectations and their betrothal to God, while witches are constrained by their pact with the Devil and bear changelings. The stigmata of the wounds of Christ on the bodies of the saints are the counterparts of the witch mole. The stigmata of Christ (pierced hands and feet, a wreath of thorns) bleed, the witch moles do not. The sufferings of the saints stand in contrast to the celebration of the witches' sabbath with its Devil worshipping. Prophecies stand in contrast to esoteric knowledge, healings to black magic, and miracles to witchcraft. The sexual life of both types of women is unusual: chastity versus excess. The saint is young, but the witch is old.

Usually the living saints began to eat less during their adolescence until they were only subsisting on water, bread and herbs. Their families and their confessors beseeched them not to refuse nourishment altogether. Many claimed to live on the host alone, which they received regularly and more often than others during Holy Communion. They held to the dogma that the body of Christ was physically present in the host, thus in turn reinforcing its credibility. These girls had generally been given a very religious upbringing by their mothers, and were expected to marry between the ages of eleven and sixteen. Most of them rebelled, took vows of chastity and usually joined a convent.

Absolute alimentary asceticism was just one of the physical constraints by means of which they desired to overcome their drives. Their lives were characterised by isolation, sleep deprivation and other excessive means of self-castigation. Saints were worshipped by the people for their supernatural and mystical abilities, especially the absence of nourishment. They were brought closer to God by ecstasies, visions, stigmata, self-castigation (some of the the saints ate worms and drank secretions of infected wounds), for example, the ability to speak prophecies and to defeat the Devil. Through excessive fasting, they also suppressed their sexual desires. Joining a convent enabled them to escape marriage and sexuality. Submission, that is self-sacrifice, also brought them closer to God's omnipotence. Self-destruction was equated with self-assertion.

People who would have been considered saints in mediaeval times were often suspected of heresy in the seventeenth century. Women who claimed a union with God while at the same time completely disregarding the Church as a mediator between God and the congregation were often regarded as members of lay communities (Habermas 1990, pp. 40–54).

Historically, the image of the saint precedes the image of the witch. The image of the witch is a complete reversal to the opposite and expresses women's desire for autonomy, self-determination and sexuality. Saints turn their aggressions, resulting from traumatic childhood experiences, against themselves, while the possessed, while turning their aggressions against themselves, seek support by exorcism and Church authority. The aggressions of those who refused to submit themselves were considered very dangerous and called witches.

The transition process from submission to God to the establishment of the individual superego and self-determined control over one's drives led to feelings of guilt and delusions of persecution. This process turned real women into witches through projective identification (see Chapter 7).

6 Psychoanalysis and History

Freud

In contemporary literature, the relation between psychoanalysis and history as a field of study appears to be a very tense one. Did Freud himself, through his theories, open the door to the antagonism towards psychoanalysis described by Peter Gay (1985), or at least contribute to the negative attitude of historians towards the application of psychoanalytic insights to historical phenomena?

For example, Freud is accused of seeing history as a form of life-history which he equates with successive infantile stages of development (Kimmerle 1998, pp. 95, 161, 172). The heterogeneity of history is obliterated and cultural-historical phenomena are included in the psychoanalytic diagnosis of individuals. The analogy of phylogeny and ontogeny would become biologically transfigured through the postulation of the inheritance of acquired characteristics in a repressed unconscious. Things that occurred in the irrevocable past, that is, experiences in man's history, are seen over the generations as the building up of traditions transgenerationally as well as in the individual unconscious. Thus, past and present decode each other. Where would this leave the criteria of truth? In Freud's theory, the history of individual understanding remains unfathomable. Past and present confirm each other. Methods and theories of the present are projected on men of the past. It is at least questionable whether such psychoanalytic interpretations lead to a better understanding of inner motives or whether they try to analyse the past from today's point of view. In Kimmerle's view, Freud interprets history as a drive-based interplay of psychology and biology.

Freud started very early to be concerned with the relationship between psychoanalysis and history. In his book *Totem and Taboo* (1912) he developed the theory of an analogy of phylogeny and ontogeny; the evolution of man from a mythical, animistic state through a religious stage to a scientific conception of the world. He later worked out in detail the different stages of evolutionary development in his book *The Future of an Illusion* (1927). Freud writes the following about the evolution of man:

" But apart from this, in a certain sense he [prehistoric man] is still our contemporary. There are men still living who, as we believe, stand very near to primitive man, far nearer than we do, and whom we therefore regard as his direct heirs and representatives. Such is our view of those whom we describe as savages or half-savages; and their mental life must have a peculiar interest for us if we are right in seeing in it a well-preserved picture of an early stage of our own development. (Freud 1927, p. 1)

Terms like 'primitive', 'savage', or 'half savage' are particularly degrading and utterly out of place in historical, cultural and ethnological works. It does not contribute to a better understanding of the text if the term 'savage tribes' of the present is used to refer to tribes of primeval times. Perhaps we should set this justified critique aside and blame it on Freud's infatuation with the concept of *Zeitgeist*. In my opinion it is more important to find out whether or not the scripts in fact support the accusations of applying faulty analogies and an ahistorical approach.

In *Totem and Taboo*, Freud reports extensively on the ethnological studies of his time, and largely draws from James Frazer's *The Golden Bough* (1910) and *Totemism and Exogamy* (1887), two critically acclaimed works in 1912. Frazer himself was a jurist who also engaged in the study of the ancient world as well as ethnological descriptions, particularly those of the aboriginal population of prehistoric Australia and Polynesia. He did not undertake any field studies himself. Freud was fascinated by the descriptions of behaviour of people in other cultures, their myths and rites. He believed he recognised the same behaviour and fears that he was familiar with from medical treatments. However, he did not simply transfer the complexes of his time – such as the form of Oedipus complex known then – to the foreign culture, but instead attempted to understand the psychic meaning of his readings, and came to some very interesting conclusions. Freud found that totemism was an unconscious way of securing the incest barrier and exogamy. Understanding this notion is not a projection of understandings from Freud's time on to earlier times. Nevertheless, Freud recognised the fear of incest in the other culture and its specific forms of rejection, also known as totemism instead of the familiar oedipal constellation. According to Freud, the basis of a totem meal is hatred and the desire for the identification of sons; worship faces unconscious hostility. The creation of religious beliefs is based on ambivalent emotions. Freud describes totemism as a religious and social system and not simply as an analogy of the psychology of individuality. He writes about ambivalence as follows:

" The prohibition owes its strength and its obsessive character precisely to its unconscious opponent, the concealed and undiminished desire – that is to say, to an internal necessity inaccessible to conscious inspection. (Freud 1912, p. 30)

He does not shrug off magic and totemism as simply superstitious, but refers to their psychic functions as the carriers of projections. Does he not in fact help increase the perceived value of foreign cultures by comprehending what is meaningful to them? Fear of incest and the idealisation of a god as a reaction formation against aggression are among the anxieties and the development tasks of people of Freud's time, and which he also recognised in other cultures. These findings are not simply projected, but perceived as culture-specific complexes, one of which is totemism.

He believed he could recognise basic feelings such as aggression, fear of incest, desire for identification, ambiguity of feelings and unconscious counter-action (later called the reaction-formation), guilt, remorse, and so on. For this reason, Freud believed in the applicability of psychoanalysis. He ascribed these basic feelings to a theory that combines inherited and acquired qualities. Freud's fascination with history and ethnology becomes comprehensible when we consider that the theory of psychoanalysis is confirmed by the fact that fears, defence mechanisms and psychic adjustment procedures are also present in history and among very different peoples.

For Freud, the inheritance of psychic affects and reaction types was by no means a question of drives, but the result of a potentially inherited disposition and acquired organisation:

" They must then have persisted from generation to generation, perhaps merely as a result of tradition transmitted through parental and social authority. Possibly, however, in later generations they may have become 'organised' as an inherited psychical endowment. Who can decide whether such things as 'innate ideas' exist, or whether in the present instance they have operated, either alone or in conjunction with education, to bring about the permanent fixing of taboos? But one thing would certainly follow from the persistence of the taboo, namely that the original desire to do the prohibited thing must also still persist among the tribes concerned. They must therefore have an ambivalent attitude towards their taboos. In their unconscious, there is nothing they would like more than to violate them, but they are afraid to do so; they are afraid precisely because they would like to, and the fear is stronger than the desire. The desire is unconscious, however, in every individual member of the tribe just as it is in neurotics. The most ancient and important taboo prohibitions are the two basic laws of totemism: not to kill the totem animal and to avoid sexual intercourse with members of the totem clan of the opposite sex. (Freud 1912, pp. 31–2)

In the psychoanalysis of today, there are numerous approaches that attempt to achieve an amalgamation of Freud's theory of basic drives and the theory of inherent affects. According to Kernberg, affects precede the drives, and self-object-affect units are primary determinants of the complete psychic structures (id, ego, superego) (Kernberg 1976, p. 57). The drives are organised only secondarily as integrating systems and are composed of units of internalised object-relations (p. 85) to an object. According to this opinion, the inherent affect dispositions constitute the primary motivational systems. Besides further inherent abilities (instinctive building blocks), they also make use of inherent perceptual and behavioural patterns (pp. 86–7).

According to Kernberg, specific affective dispositions and internalised object-relations determine the structures of the drives as either 'good' or 'bad' affects. Inherent affect dispositions colour object-relations. Since the ego is weak, affect dispositions are initially split into 'good' and 'bad'. It is out of these affect dispositions and the actual experience of different interactions, that is, the formation of differentiated self-representations and object representations, that the libido and aggression are structured.

" Affects represent inborn dispositions to a subjective experience in the dimension of pleasure and unpleasure; that they are activated simultaneously with inborn behaviour patterns, which elicit reciprocal environmental (mothering) reactions, and with general arousal, which increases the perception of external and internal stimuli occurring during this interaction; and that all of this leads to the fixation of memory traces in a primitive, 'affective memory' constellation or unit incorporating self components, object components, and the affect state itself ... Pleasurable and painful affects are the major organisers of the series of 'good' and 'bad' internalised object relations and constitute the major motivational or drive systems which organise intra-psychic experience. Libido and aggression are not external givens in this development, but represent the overall organisation of drive systems in the general polarity of 'good' and 'bad'. Affect states first determine the integration of both internalised object relations and the overall drive systems; ... Libido and aggression represent the two overall psychic structures which integrate instinctive components and the other building blocks first consolidated in units of internalised object relations. (Kernberg 1976, p. 104)

In the field of infant research, the reduction of affect dispositions to merely 'good' and 'bad' is regarded as too narrow. It provides approaches which no longer rule out the explanation of an inherent affect disposition by means of psychoanalytic theory (Krause 1983, Lichtenberg 1983, Stern 1990). From this perspective, the reproaches brought against Freud for basing his findings on a simple theory of inheritance are hardly sustainable. Is it not more likely that he anticipated the questions we deal with today? Affect dispositions and drives develop in complicated, culturally different variations and forms of defence by means of internalised interactional experience. Genetics does not rule out historic and cultural differences.

Freud found the affect of ambivalence in adoration and idolisation and the taboo of royalty to be one which is unconsciously opposed by an intensely hostile attitude. He acknowledges that there are differences between various cultural epochs as far as ambivalence is concerned. In every culture, affect is dealt with in different ways:

" In maintaining the essential similarity between taboo prohibitions and moral prohibitions, I have not sought to dispute the fact that there must be a psychological difference between them. The only possible reason why the prohibitions no longer take the form of taboos must be some change in the circumstances governing the ambivalence underlying them. (Freud 1912, p. 71)

Although Freud learned to understand affects while treating patients, he noticed the difference between neurosis and affects which he thought he perceived in historical phenomena:

" In our analytical examination of the problems of taboo, we have hitherto allowed ourselves to be led by the points of agreement that we have been able to show between it and obsessional neurosis. But, after all, taboo is not a neurosis but a social institution. We are therefore faced with the task of explaining what difference there is in principle between a neurosis and a cultural creation such as taboo. (Freud 1912, p. 71)

It is certainly more problematic that Freud judges the historical development merely as progress, and that he compares it to advancement in personal development, going along with the authors he refers to, thus following the *Zeitgeist*. Of course, historians cannot accept this perception of the earlier evolutionary periods as being the childhood of mankind:

" If we may regard the existence among primitive races of the omnipotence of thoughts as evidence in favour of narcissism, we are encouraged to attempt a comparison between the phases in the development of men's view of the universe and the stages of an individual's libidinal development. The animistic phase would correspond to narcissism, both chronologically and in its content; the religious phase would correspond to the stage of object-choice of which the characteristic is a child's attachment to his parents; while the scientific phase would have an exact counterpart in the stage at which an individual has reached maturity, has renounced the pleasure principle, adjusted himself to reality and turned to the external world for the object of his desires. (Freud 1912, p. 90)

If the problem of applying psychoanalysis to historical epochs and different cultures is not so much a question of general applicability (if we do not want to assume that people living in different times and in different cultural areas have a completely different psychic disposition, and at the moment there does not appear to be any evidence to support this theory), then the question of what is interpreted by psychoanalysis arises. How have the historical or ethnological conclusions been drawn? Are they perhaps already distorted? This leads to the necessity of a historical or ethnological foundation for psychoanalytic findings. Is it not only by means of a thorough description of historical and ethnological phenomena that a psychoanalytic interpretation that has not been seriously distorted by projections of one's own cultural background can be reached? Psychoanalytic interpretation depends on a thorough historical study of sources or field research. It is necessary for the analyst to use self-reflection and the analysis of counter-transference to achieve a culture-specific understanding of the historical source text. Freud mentions his criticism of the methods of achieving findings in a neglected footnote, but, unfortunately, he does not elaborate that thought in his writings. He writes:

" It may be as well, however, to warn the reader in advance of the difficulties with which any statements on the subject have to contend. In the first place, those who collect the observations are not the same as those who examine and discuss them. The former are travellers and missionaries while the latter are students who may never have set eyes on the objects of their researches. Again, communication with savages is not an easy matter. The observers are not always acquainted with the native language but may be obliged to rely on the help of interpreters or to conduct their inquiries through the medium of pidgin-English. Savages are not communicative on the subject of the most intimate details of their cultural life and they talk openly only to those foreigners who have lived among them for many years. They often give false or misleading information for a great variety of motives. It should not be forgotten that primitive races are not young races, but are in fact as old as civilised races. There is no reason to suppose that, for the benefit of our information, they have retained their original ideas and institutions undeveloped and undistorted. On the contrary, it is certain that there have been profound changes in every direction among primitive races, so that it is never possible to decide without hesitation how far their present-day conditions and opinions preserve the primeval past in a petrified form and how far they are distortions and modifications of it. Hence arise the all-too-frequent disputes among the authorities as to which characteristics of a primitive civilisation are to be regarded as primary and as to which are later and secondary developments. The determination of the original state of things thus invariably remains a matter of construction. Finally, it is not easy to feel one's way into primitive modes of thinking. We misunderstand primitive men just as easily as we do children, and we are always apt to interpret their actions and feelings according to our own mental constellations. (Freud 1912, pp. 102–3)

The application of psychoanalytic findings depends on the acquired ethnological or historical findings. After all, distortion of the perceptions can also occur secondarily. Freud considers totemism as a father religion:

" If the totem animal is the father, then the two principal ordinances of totemism, the two taboo prohibitions which constitute its core – not to kill the totem and not to have sexual relations with a woman of the same totem – coincide in their content with the two crimes of Oedipus, who killed his father and married his mother, as well as with the two primal wishes of children, the insufficient repression or the re-awakening of which forms the nucleus of perhaps every psychoneurosis. (Freud 1912, p. 132)

According to Freud, totemism resulted from the rebellion of the sons against the father.

" Totemic religion arose from the filial sense of guilt, in an attempt to allay that feeling and to appease the father by deferred obedience to him. All later religions are seen to be attempts at solving the same problem. They vary according to the stage of civilisation at which they arise and according to the methods which they adopt; but all have the same end in view and are reactions to the same great event with which civilisation began and which, since it occurred, has not allowed mankind a moment's rest. (Freud 1912, p. 145)

My own research in the totemistic, matrilineal culture of Micronesia (Heinemann 1995) shows that the totem gods form male and female couples, enabling an analogous development for boys and girls, who are entrusted at the age of six to the age-homogeneous group, that is, the men's or women's club. Being a member of either the men's or women's club with its sex-specific tasks and political organisations stabilises sexual identity and sets the stage for the separation/individuation process from the mother. On a more general level, that of the structuring of sexual identity and the establishment of the incest taboo, the rituals correspond to the tasks which (in our culture) are assumed by the Oedipus complex. The sexual identity in the culture I studied is maintained through social separation: men and women are not allowed to eat together and belong to the separated men's and women's respective social groups. Considering these findings, Freud would have projected only patriarchal distortion, not the whole Oedipus complex of his time – the three-person-family structure. The emphasis on the father–son conflict seems to be a typical Freudian fixation, a feature of his time. In the totemistic culture of Micronesia, it is not the father but the siblings who lead the clan. Only careful ethnological research in conjunction with psychoanalytic theory and self-reflection on the part of the analyst make insight possible. Unfortunately, Freud did not continue along the path he mentioned in the footnote.

In his work, *The Future of an Illusion* (1927), Freud considers historical development exclusively as progress towards a scientific way of thinking and reasoning. This development is supposed to be based on increasing strengthening of the superego, as was shown in that study. But we could also see what kind of aggressions were released during this development, so that Freud's optimism can at least be called into question, at least from a historical point of view. With regard to this development, Freud writes:

" It is not true that the human mind has undergone no development since the earliest times and that, in contrast to the advances of science and technology, it is the same to-day as it was at the beginning of history. We can point out one of these mental advances at once. It is in keeping with the course of human development that external coercion gradually becomes internalised; for a special mental agency, man's super-ego, takes it over and includes it among its commandments. (Freud 1927, p. 11)

According to Freud, the increasing power of the superego is an extremely valuable psychological possession of a culture. Since nature threatens people with dangers, they have joined together and created culture. Freud sees the first step in this progress in the humanisation of nature. In nature, when one is surrounded by those who are familiar, one can breathe freely, feel at home in unfamiliar surroundings and can psychically cope with irrational fears. According to Freud, this situation is not new: it has already been experienced in childhood. In its state of helplessness, the child could rely on its parents, who usually offered their protection. The two situations were adapted to each other.

Man transformed nature into deities to ban its horrors and to be compensated for all the pain and hardship that culture brought upon him. According to Freud, the emphasis changed as time passed – man recognised the independence of the laws of nature. In this later work, Freud regarded human impotence and helplessness as being essential for the creation of religion. In his opinion, the forces of nature were personifed according to the infantile model in order to rule nature.

" I believe rather that when man personifies the forces of nature, he is again following an infantile model. He has learnt from the people present in his earliest environment that the way to influence them is to establish a relation with them; and so, later on, with the same end in view, he treats everything else that he comes across in the same way as he treated those persons. Thus I do not contradict your descriptive observation; it is in fact natural to man to personify everything that he wants to understand in order later to control it (psychical mastering as a preparation for physical mastering); but I provide in addition a motive and a genesis for this peculiarity of human thinking. (Freud 1927, p. 22)

Freud now regards the development of culture completely under the aspect of the strengthening of the superego – a development from submitting to religious norms towards their internalisation.

" It is doubtful whether men were in general happier at a time when religious doctrines held unrestricted sway; more moral they certainly were not. They have always known how to externalise the precepts of religion and thus to nullify their intentions. (Freud 1927, p. 37)

According to Freud, man sinned, then made a sacrifice or did penitence and was then free to sin again. Thus the superego is more powerful than subservience to religion.

> If this view is right, it is to be supposed that a turning-away from religion is bound to occur with the fatal inevitability of a process of growth, and that we find ourselves at this very juncture in the middle of that phase of development. (Freud 1927, p. 43)

The analysis of the witch persecution period seems to confirm Freud's theory of the position of the superego development. But does 'early' also have to mean 'less mature'? When we examine the dimensions of aggression which are released through this development, the question arises of whether Freud was idealising. After all, for a long time Freud underestimated or perhaps even denied the aggressions of his time. However, on the other hand, the idealisation of the past is just as unsatisfactory.

Freud sees the historical value of religious theories for the psychic development, now the rational, intellectual effort should follow. He declared that the only intention of his writing was to draw attention to the necessity of this progress: reality-orientated education and the realisation of the satisfying and comforting power of the illusion of religion.

> The voice of the intellect is a soft one, but it does not rest till it has gained a hearing. Finally, after a countless succession of rebuffs, it succeeds. (Freud 1927, p. 53)

According to Freud, nothing can resist reason and experience in the long run. They eventually come into open conflict with religion:

> We believe that it is possible for scientific work to gain some knowledge about the reality of the world, by means of which we can increase our power and in accordance with which we can arrange our life. If this belief is an illusion, then we are in the same position as you. But science has given us evidence by its numerous and important successes that it is no illusion. (Freud 1927, p. 55)

In *Civilization and its Discontents* (1930), Freud deals further with the question of the analogy between cultural processes and individual development.

> When, however, we look at the relationship between the process of human civilisation and the developmental or educational process of individual human beings, we have to conclude without much hesitation that the two are very similar in nature, if not the very same process applied to different kinds of objects. (Freud 1930, pp. 139–40).

In Freud's opinion, the main characteristic of individual development is the egoistic striving for happiness, while that of cultural development is usually restriction. The development process of the individual has special features which cannot be found in the cultural process of mankind. The analogy between the cultural process and the development of the individual within a community forms the super-ego, which has a strong influence on cultural development. Freud considers the superego of a cultural period to have a similar origin as the superego of the individual human being. He regards the superego as the link between cultural and individual development, and stresses that the latter superego is not necessarily the stricter one.

" As regards the primitive peoples who exist to-day, careful researches have shown that their instinctual life is by no means to be envied for its freedom. It is subject to restrictions of a different kind but perhaps of greater severity than those attaching to modern civilised man. (Freud 1930, p. 115)

The severity of the superego depends on the extent to which aggressive impulses are suppressed. This finding was significant during the time of the witch persecutions.

" But the essential difference is that the original severity of the super-ego does not – does not so much – represent the severity which one has experienced from it (the object), or which one attributes to it; it represents rather one's own aggressiveness towards it. If this is correct, we may assert truly that in the beginning conscience arises through the suppression of an aggressive impulse, and that it is subsequently reinforced by fresh suppressions of the same kind. (Freud 1930, pp. 129–30)

However, Freud also realised that this analogy can only be pursued to a limited extent.

" The process of the civilisation of the human species is, of course, an abstraction of a higher order than is the development of the individual and it is therefore harder to apprehend in concrete terms, nor should we pursue analogies to an obsessional extreme; but in view of the similarity between the aims of the two processes – in the one case the integration of a separate individual into a human group, and in the other case the creation of a unified group out of many individuals – we can not be surprised at the similarity between the means employed and the resultant phenomena. (Freud 1930, p. 140)

In *Moses and Monotheism* (1938), Freud again deals with the issue of the heredity of psychic memory traces:

" We cannot at first sight say in what form this past existed during the time of its eclipse. It is not easy for us to carry over the concepts of individual psychology into group psychology; and I do not think we gain anything by introducing the concept of a 'collective' unconscious. The content of the unconscious, indeed, is in any case a collective, universal property of mankind. For the moment, then, we will make shift with the use of analogies. The processes in the life of peoples which we are studying here are very similar to those familiar to us in psychopathology, but nevertheless not quite the same. We must finally make up our minds to adopt the hypothesis that the psychical precipitates of the primeval period became inherited property which, in each fresh generation, called not for acquisition but only for awakening. (Freud 1938, p. 132)

" If we assume the survival of these memory-traces in the archaic heritage, we have bridged the gulf between individual and group psychology: we can deal with peoples as we do with an individual neurotic. Granted that at the time we have no stronger evidence for the presence of memory-traces in the archaic heritage than the residual phenomena of the work of analysis which call for a phylogenetic derivation, yet this evidence seems to us strong enough to postulate that such is the fact. (Freud 1938, p. 100)

Although he accepts the concept of heredity, Freud does not go so far as to denigrate or mitigate the significance of cultural variations:

" The return of the repressed took place slowly and certainly not spontaneously but under the influence of all the changes in conditions of life which fill the history of human civilisation. (Freud 1938, p. 133)

As not all experiences of the primeval period are passed down, Freud explains the conditions under which an experience follows 'the way of the archaic heritage': the psychic affect must have been important enough and must have occurred repeatedly. It will finally become active, that is to say, conscious, by recent, actual repetition, resulting in the return of what has been suppressed.

Unfortunately, Freud did not go on to pursue the idea of investigating reality by means of the concept he presented in a footnote to *Totem and Taboo*. His later works increasingly emphasise his belief in progress and the role of the archaic heritage.

According to Brunner (1996), Freud neglects the importance of the socio-economic factors involved in producing collective fears as well as the destructive effects of fantasies of political omnipotence. Although he wrote about the origins and effects of powerlessness in history, he not only ignored the sources and the intensity of these feelings in his own society, but also the disastrous collective pathology. He turned his back on the actual situation of his time. In his attempt to give a scientific explanation of the origins and function of religion – an explanation which was intended to emancipate mankind from religion and destroy the myth of God – he even developed mythical categories of explanation, for example:

- the assumption that acquired qualities are passed on throughout history and between cultures
- the postulate of a castrating primal man who turned into the archetype of all fathers
- the supposition that far-reaching patricide (because of incest) actually did occur
- the assumption that a collective unconscious exists in which the memory of the original crime and a general feeling of guilt are preserved.

According to Brunner, there are social phenomena which can be reasonably described as collective pathologies even if Freud virtually created a political myth. However, they have to be examined thoroughly through historical research. Psychoanalysis also has to deal with and incorporate real power.

By citing Freud's analysis of witch persecutions, I would like to illustrate the importance of thorough, historical research as a precondition for psychoanalytic interpretation.

Freud's thoughts on possession, the fear of witches and hysteria are based on three historical errors.

According to Freud, the witch persecutions took place during the Middle Ages. From a historical point of view, however, the sixteenth and seventeenth centuries belong to the Early Modern Age. It is probably due to these errors that the connection to substantial changes of the superego was overlooked.

Freud believed that the women accused of being witches were possessed and, following Charcot's tradition (1886), he saw them as being merely hysterical. This is another interpretation based on a lack of historical knowledge, because the possessed women were, as I tried to show in my study, normally not referred to as witches. Freud writes:

" In the Middle Ages neuroses played a significant part in the history of civilisation, they appeared in epidemics as a result of psychical contagion, and were at the root of what was factual in the history of possession and of witchcraft. (Freud 1888, p. 41)

In a letter to Fliess on 17 January 1897, Freud wrote:

" What would you say, by the way, if I told you that all of my brand-new prehistory of hysteria is already known and was published a hundred times over, though several centuries ago? Do you remember that I always said that the medieval theory of possession held by the ecclesiastical courts was identical with our theory of a foreign body and the splitting of consciousness? (Freud 1985, p. 224)

Freud did not consider the fact that the witch, unlike the possessed woman, is not overpowered by strange forces, but turns deliberately to evil forces. Freud considered both of them hysterical. Possession, witchcraft and hysteria were all the same for Freud. In his opinion, only the reactions to these women were different during the Middle Ages and in his time. This was due to an interpretation first based on the demonological and then on the medical point of view.

" During the last few decades a hysterical woman would have been almost as certain to be treated as a malingerer, as in earlier centuries she would have been certain to be judged and condemned as a witch or as possessed of the devil. (Freud 1956, p. 11)

The stigmata diaboli then were hysterogenic zones. 'The Middle Ages had a precise acquaintance with the "stigmata" of hysteria, its somatic signs, and interpreted and made use of them in their own fashion' (Freud 1956, p. 11). For Freud, this was the proof that 'the identity of hysteria at every time and place was insisted upon' (p. 13), and 'that their symptomatology has undergone no change up to the present day' (p. 41), unlike the interpretation of them. 'A proper assessment and a better understanding of the disease only began with the works of Charcot and of the school of the Salpêtrière inspired by him', says Freud (1888, p. 41).

Charcot considered possession by demons a religious misinterpretation of a medically explicable fact. He considered the possessed woman to be hysterical. The demonological approach is dismissed as an expression of the unenlightened, unknowing period of history, as a turning-point from the theological to the medical pattern of interpretation. Witches and possessed women were reinterpreted as hysterics, wrongly associated with demonically ill people because of a religious craze.

We see that Freud's belief in the progress of human development led to historical misinterpretations. As Freud misinterpreted possessed women as witches, he finally comes to the third historical shortcoming of his interpretation. He interprets the torture imposed by the witches' judges as a precursor of psychoanalytic treatment. In the above-mentioned letter to Fliess, Freud asks: 'But why did the Devil who took possession of the poor things invariably abuse them sexually and in a loathsome manner? Why are their confessions under torture so like the communications made by my patients in psychic treatment?' (Freud 1985, p. 224).

The needles spat out by the witches (as already mentioned, Freud did not distinguish between possessed persons and witches), Freud considered as a part of the process of seduction, but at the same time the hysterical woman would be afraid of being pricked. 'Once more, the inquisitors prick with needles to discover the Devil's stigmata, and in a similar situation the victims think of the same old cruel story in fictionalized form (helped perheps [sic] by disguises of the seducers). Thus, not only the victims but also the executioners recalled in this their earliest youth' (Freud 1985, p. 225). The seduction by the Devil is considered here as an oedipal fantasy. The witches' judges Freud looked upon as victims of that kind of fantasy. The fantasies of the witches are interpreted as oedipal seduction. The witch's broom could be seen as a symbol for the penis. Freud even felt he had found vestiges of a very old sexual cult in the symptoms: 'I dream, therefore, of a primeval Devil religion with rites that are carried on secretly, and understand the harsh therapy of the witches' judges' (p. 227).

It seems that Freud was not overly concerned about the contradiction of using a psychotherapeutic practice with inquisitional means to elicit confessions. Freud considered the psychotherapist and the witches' judge to be in the same position; one could even say that psychoanalysis entered into the heritage of the 'strict therapy of the witches' judges'. The strange similarity of the confessions made by his patients and by tortured persons, in Freud's opinion simply reflected the fact that the same past (oedipal fantasies) is represented in them. In both cases resistance would have to be broken that was preventing hidden things from being brought to the surface.

A more exact historical analysis would, however, have had led to different results. If we distinguish between possessed persons and women accused of being witches, it was not the torture itself that was the precursor of the psychoanalytic therapy, but the exorcism.

I think that the comparison to the immense effort made for the possessed women during the procedure of exorcism is more appropriate to the psychoanalytic method. Was it Freud's belief in progress that made him shut his eyes to this almost incredible thought?

I will later go into more detail regarding the question of oedipal fantasies of the possessed and the witch accusers (Chapter 7). The one-sided interpretation of the Freudian theory of seduction in favour of oedipal fantasies turns the tortured into perpetrators. Contrary to Freud, Lorenzer (1984), who described the history of psychoanalysis from exorcism to Freud, stresses the fundamental difference between torture and the method of psychoanalysis. 'The *folie à deux* rapport between the victim and the inquisitor was the infernal oppositional image of that which would later characterise Psychoanalysis. The space for free self-representation – later to become the key feature of psychoanalysis – here assumes the absence of freedom represented by a forced staging resulting from the inquisition. Instead of the intimate interlocking of transference and counter-transference, there is the forced rapport between the victim and the inquisitor' (Lorenzer 1984, p. 45). A forced adaptation of a certain role was only noticeable during the witchcraft trails, not during the persecutions set off by the possessed. According to Lorenzer, the possessed played an active role and provoked the comparison with hysteria. This is the reason for the development of the term hysterodaemonopathia in the nineteenth century. The view of possession as a medical phenomenon became common in the eighteenth century. The exorcist and priest Johann Josef Gassner, who treated many with his incantations under the sign of the cross in 1774, and the physician Franz Anton Messmer (1734–1815) with his magnetic therapy, paved the way for hypnosis, Charcot and Freud.

Psychoanalysis and Historians

Up to the present, psychoanalysis is not very popular in historical research. Despite several attempts to bring it closer to history, the interest of historians in psychoanalysis is still restricted, although it is obvious that it is not sufficient to look only at conscious conflicts of interest if one studies historical phenomena. There are often no rational explanations for historical processes but only superficial rationalisations behind which something else is hidden (Kimmerle 1998, p. 77).

The historian Peter Gay (1985) describes the situation in a drastic and dramatic way. Most historians would have reacted with anxiety and pure rage to attempts to draw psychoanalysis into the study of history. These historians argued that a person who looks at the past with a psychoanalytic knowledge offends common sense, ignores the relevance of or fails to recognise the sparseness of the source material. By nature, psychoanalysis is ahistorical, because it starts from the assumption of the unchangeable nature of human beings, which contradicts the interest of the historian in the development and profound modification of this nature. They would claim that Freud's conception of man is a generalisation of the Viennese bourgeoisie from the turn of the century, and that psychoanalysis has failed miserably in the field of historiography. On the basis of his own experience, Gay states that anyone who tries to include psychoanalysis into the study of history will meet with massive resistance (Gay 1985, pp. 5–8).

Even more drastically, Gay writes that psychohistory can be declared a disaster area. The historians' guild has sealed itself off to psychoanalysis. The main points of criticism, he says, are its unreflected handling of source material and its penchant for reductionism (Gay 1985, pp. 16–17).

Finally, Gay says, Freud is misrepresented out of ignorance and consequently rejected. First he was misinterpreted and then dismissed: 'These historians have made things easy for themselves; by making nonsense of Freud, they have had no trouble demonstrating that Freud is talking nonsense' (Gay 1985, p. 31).

However, Gay considers psychoanalysis to be helpful for understanding historical contexts which could not be understood otherwise. Thus, psychoanalysis can be applied to historical events because drives have different vicissitudes. This means that they are determined to a great extent by the cultural milieu and are transferred within the self to psychic representations (Gay 1985, p. 91). According to him, the same mixture of plasticity and affinity also characterises the mechanisms of defence which are a second constant factor of human life. Mechanisms of defence constitute a joint experience in dealing with conflicts occurring in astonishing but not unlimited variety. If there were not something like human nature, no general laws could be established in history. The most revealing and most problematic conflict is the Oedipus complex. The standard version is only the starting point for the analyst; there are different solutions for different times and cultures.

" Doubtless the most interesting building blocks for such a history are what Anna Freud called the mechanisms of defence. They are so interesting because, though deeply personal psychological manoeuvres, they are chiefly developed in response to collective external realities, and remain in continuous and close touch with them. Ubiquitous, versatile, inventive, these unconscious stratagems make civilisation possible and bearable. (Gay 1985, p. 163)

Gay states that drives are not fixed behavioural dispositions, but are generally put on social tracks and reshaped by society. As I have proposed, Gay also takes the fundamental concepts of psychoanalysis as a starting point, which have to be studied in their historical form. It is no coincidence that – like Freud – Gay speaks of ethnology in this context, specifically the Oedipus complex on the Trobriand Islands (Gay 1985, p. 98). The fate of individuals makes it possible to interpret the entirety of culture, but this depends on a careful investigation of the social milieu. Gay also comes to the conclusion that it was not so much a matter of the application of psychoanalysis to historical phenomena in principle, but a matter of the diligence of historical and psychoanalytic research, as I did in my criticism of Freud. The expeditions of the psychoanalysts into psychohistory have only been partially convincing. 'It is certainly undeniable that the record Freudian historians, beginning with Freud himself, have compiled is less than confidence-inspiring' (p. 182).

According to Gay, historians who included psychoanalysis into their studies were also deceived by the same reductionism and did not by any means include sufficient psychoanalytic research results. Nevertheless, Gay argues that psychoanalysis should be used as an additional resource for historical research.

" Life, as the historian studies it, whether in the individual or the group, in single events or long sweeps of time, is a series of compromises in which the irrepressible drives, the warning signals of anxiety, the stratagems of defence, the persecutions of the superego, all play a leading but not an exclusive role. History is more than a monologue of the unconscious, more than a dance of symptoms. (Gay 1985, p. 211)

Brumberg's book, *Fasting Girls* (1988), serves here as an example of psychoanalytically insufficient historical work. Brumberg describes as hysterical those young girls of the Middle Ages who were considered living saints due to their eating behaviour. Without examining it in any psychoanalytic respect, Brumberg considers the *anorexia mirabilis* to be a form of hysteria.

In my opinion, another psychoanalytically insufficient historical work is that of the Australian historian, Lyndal Roper, entitled *Oedipus and the Devil* (1994). Roper has made a broad attempt to apply psychoanalytic theory to the phenomenon of witch persecutions. Unfortunately, she sticks entirely to Freud's theses and so her work will necessarily contribute to the increased resentment of academic historians. In trying to apply Freud's theses in a historical context at all costs, Roper makes psychoanalytically as well as historically grotesque statements. Like Freud, she does not differentiate between possessed women and witches. Finally, she even tries to consider torture as a therapy. Freud's comment on the witches' judges now becomes the central point which Roper tries to prove. Roper assumes that in the witches' confessions made under torture, their unconscious is expressed. Although she admits that the women were violently forced to these confessions, she states at the same time that the tortured victims expressed their own convictions. 'Our evidence for their beliefs derives from their interrogations conducted at first without and then with the application of torture' (Roper 1994, p. 82).

Now the confession is even turned into a creative performance carried out by the witch:

" Witchcraft confessions have often been understood as the projections of a male-dominated society. But this is to ignore the creative work which the witch herself carried out, translating her own life experiences into the language of the diabolic, performing her own diabolic theatre. The fantasies she wove, though often forced from her through torture, were her own condensations of shared cultural preoccupations. (Roper 1994, p. 20)

Torture is reinterpreted almost as a therapeutic conversation:

" Their judges and scribes noted all this with fascinated attention. And in this way witches themselves carried out cultural work, creating the narrative of the witch anew, making sense of emotions and cultural process. Willing or not, witchcraft trials are one context in which women 'speak' at greater length and receive more attention than perhaps any other. (Roper 1994, p. 20)

Roper ignores the compulsion of torture as well as people's fear of witches. Torture is considered to be self-healing of the tortured person. Roper can only come to this conclusion because she – like Freud – does not distinguish between the possessed, who normally accuse themselves, and the women accused of being witches. This distinction is significant, because the reactions to possessed people and witches were completely different. Attempts were made to heal the possessed through exorcism, whereas witches were tortured and executed.

The fantasies confessed to under torture are not seen as the dynamics of interrogation in which the inquisitors forced their concepts on the interrogated women, but at the same time, they agreed with the women's phantasms because they belonged to the same culture. By means of repeated torture details were confirmed and inconsistencies were examined until finally no more doubt about the confession remained. Nevertheless, Roper continues: 'It was a truth which the witch herself freely acknowledged and for which she alone had provided the material' (Roper 1994, p. 205). Torture became a means of creating meaning. 'But narratives in which people try to make sense of their psychic conflicts usually involve borrowing from a language which is not at first the individual's own' (p. 206).

Then it is even possible 'to discern the ways in which the sadism of the questioning process may have gratified the needs of the witch' (Roper 1994, p. 229). The court of the Inquisition becomes a stage on which the witch is acting out her inner conflicts:

> Interrogation for witchcraft, we might say, offered the accused a theatrical opportunity to recount and restage these linked conflicts – and what better audience than the rapt ears of the council's representatives and the executioner. (Roper 1994, p. 232)

If Roper was referring to the exorcisms she actually knows about, one could agree with her to some extent. However, the interrogation is played down to a conversation in which the witch talks about her psychic problems: 'Her narrative was the product of a conversation' (Roper 1994, p. 234). Thus the compulsion exerted on her is interpreted in another way: 'In the figure of the Devil, the witch had available to her a character who could dramatise psychic conflicts with extraordinary clarity' (p. 233). Again, Roper actually describes the possessed women and not the witches, as she believes.

She goes so far as to state that she sees a pattern of family relationships in the interrogation: 'If we look at the interaction in the interrogation, we notice that much of it dramatises relations between fathers and daughters' (Roper 1994, p. 235). The confession becomes an action controlled by the witch herself in the course of which she manages 'to play the drama of the disobedient daughter' (p. 239). Roper interprets the inquisitors' torture as a kind of assistance for the witch who is put under pressure by their questions:

> Elements in the interaction between the witch and her persecutors allowed the fantasy of witchcraft to unfold. The psychic conflicts attendant on the feminine position – whether oedipal or related to motherhood – provided the substance of the psychic drama of the witchcraft interrogation, and supplied the material on which their interrogators could work in fascinated horror, developing in turn their own fantasies about femininity, about fatherhood and about diabolic activity. (Roper 1994, p. 240)

According to Roper, the witch expressed oedipal fantasies when tortured, the torturers became oedipal objects and torture itself gave her mental relief:

" Like a kind of medicine of salvation, it assisted her travail to return to the Christian community in contrition so that she might die in a state of grace. Torture was part of an understanding, shared by the witch and her persecutors, of the interrelation of body and soul: the skin of the outer person had to be flayed away to arrive at psychological truth. Those who did not crack under torture were set free despite the seriousness of the accusations against them, because they were said to have proven their innocence: they lacked a diabolic interiority of this kind. (Roper 1994, pp. 203–4)

" In this sadistic game of showing and concealing, the witch forced her persecutors to apply and reapply pain, prising her body apart to find her secret. (Roper 1994, p. 206)

Once accused, it is a fact that witches had almost no chance to survive the interrogations. Nevertheless, Roper fails to recognise this historical material in order to prove the theory of the witches' oedipal fantasies. In my opinion this serious misunderstanding occurs because she uses the case of a girl called Regina as documentary material for her thesis. In accordance with my analysis of the case study, Regina has to be seen as a child witness. These children were neglected and/or sexually abused and therefore *did* need the help of a court hearing in order to accuse culprits on behalf of the Devil fantasies and to get psychic relief. Regina's mother had numerous affairs and was banished for adultery. At the age of twelve, Regina had her first affair with a prison guard who was much older than herself. Roper considers this the realisation of an oedipal fantasy (Roper 1994, p. 232). Like most child witnesses, Regina maintained that the Devil himself had seduced her (p. 231). In Roper's view, Regina's self-accusation was her way of accusing the men who seduced and used her, and of taking her revenge on them. Roper interprets the girl's behaviour as an expression of oedipal desire. Hence, victims turn into culprits, which is the consequence of a one-sided interpretation of Freudian seduction theory.

According to Roper, Regina's case points out the self-destructive potential that witches harbour. Regina brought about her own imprisonment. A decisive feature of Regina's trial was her drive to blame herself, to be punished and to reveal the truth about the crime she was convinced she had committed (Roper 1994, p. 229). On the one hand, Roper believes that:

" The summary of Regina Bartholome's relations with the Devil with which I began this chapter was not a free initial admission. It emerged, with considerable resistance, over the course of eight sessions of interrogation both with and without torture and its threat. (Roper 1994, p. 230)

On the other hand, she states that:

" This was an extraordinary, voluntary admission, not a response to a question. It was Regina herself who brought the Devil into the story, explaining how he had visited her in her cell when she had first been imprisoned by the Council. (Roper 1994, p. 230)

Regina should not be considered a witch, but rather a tragic example of a child witness. Her first seducer was a prison guard. She wanted him to be punished. She maintains that he was the Devil. Roper explains that the sexual seduction was thus transformed into an oedipal fantasy: Regina believed that she deserved to be punished, because she had put her oedipal fantasies into practice by getting in her father's love and taking her mother's place, while keeping the house and cooking for her father (Roper 1994, p. 232).

The Devil acted as a guardian for Regina, as he did for several child witnesses in her situation. Like Regina, the Devil was fond of lung sausage and beer. He was always elegantly dressed. Regina had renounced her faith and accepted the Devil as her father. At the same time he was her lover. He was able to seduce her because she was lecherous and after money. The Devil was the good father who gave Regina sausage, money and love. But he was also unreliable. The money he gave her was counterfeit, and he beat her in the cell. From a psychoanalytic point of view, cause and consequence are confounded here. I think that the sexual seduction experienced at the age of twelve together with the looming threat of incest is the main reason behind the inner conflict that triggered Regina's defence mechanism of sexualisation. Regina does not take the Devil as her father of her own free will, but because of inner conflicts which force her to defend her oedipal fantasies in this form. With the defence mechanism of sexualisation Regina shows now sexualised behaviour herself and is supported by the Devil. Sexual abuse or the fear of sexual harassment are defended by the fantasy of being the Devil's bride. While in reality she was the victim who was not able to defend herself, in her fantasy and, perhaps secondarily, even in reality she is the offender who actively looks for sexuality. The Devil fantasy is therefore a product of defence and not, as Roper thinks, the expression of simple oedipal wishes. Goldberg (1975) describes the defence mechanism of sexualisation. By turning from passivity to activity, traumatic experiences are worked out psychically via sexualisation:

" The passive experience of being overcome by painful affects – not merely anxiety but clearly delineated feeling states – is handled by sexualising the entire situation which then can be tolerated or mastered in this active sexual manner. (Goldberg 1975, p. 337)

According to Goldberg, even the anticipation of mental pain, and not only the experience of sexual abuse can lead to sexualisation, which introduces new impulses into the discussion of the Freudian theory of seduction (cf. Chapter 7).

Regina was not 'cured' by religious education like the other child witnesses due to the unfortunate mixing with elements of the *maleficium*. Under torture she confessed that the Devil had asked her to get poison, that she had tried to set two houses on fire and to poison the bride of the man with whom she was in love. In my opinion, Regina was executed because under torture she recounted fantasies that differed from sexual seduction by the Devil and because she expressed her aggressive wishes and fantasies. These self-accusations of the child witnesses can be seen as an attempt at self-healing in Roper's sense, but not the witch trials. People's reactions in the seventeenth century show that they felt the difference. Usually, child witnesses were subject to compulsory conversion.

According to Roper, accusations of witchcraft have always been based on deep hostility between women despite the emphasis on witches' oedipal fantasies. This contradicts the historical findings cited in my work: About 80 per cent of the prosecutors were men (Weber 1996, p. 63). Demos also states that the majority of the witches' victims were male: 'Young men supplied a far larger number of victims than any other category' (Demos 1982, p. 157).

Despite this, Roper tries to prove her theory of pre-oedipal envy. The main focus was placed on things connected with sucking, childbirth, feeding and caring, the physical condition of women who had just given birth, and the susceptibility of newly born infants (Roper 1994, p. 202). The mothers' accusations were of pre-oedipal character, that is to say, they dealt with the child's relationship to the mother and the female breast. Envy dates back to this early stage, too.

" Witchcraft accusations followed a pattern with a psychic logic: the accusations were made by women who experienced childbirth, and their most common type of target was a post-menopausal, infertile woman who was caring for the infant. Often, as in the case we have just explored, she was the lying-in-maid. (Roper 1994, p. 203)

According to Roper, the witches' *maleficium* caused deformations of babies: mutilated legs, strange marks on the body, the child's suffering or its death. The soil on which such rumours of witchcraft could grow was the mother's grief for having lost her precious baby. Roper asks why motherhood allows such murderous hostility between women. She answers her own question by stating that the defence mechanism of splitting which causes the mother to consider herself exclusively a good mother and projects the negative feelings toward the other mother; the lying-in-maid is her answer to the latter question. She was made for playing the part of the evil mother. The new mother recalled early childhood memories relating to the frightening dependence on her own mother. The lying-in-maid was too old, infertile, and without a husband. She posed a double threat to the mother since she also embodied a sexual danger. If the husband had bad intentions the lying-in maids often gave birth to illegitimate children and, as a consequence were suspected of having seduced the husband (Roper 1994, pp. 202–3).

With respect to my study, it seems very improbable that the women accused of being witches were mainly lying-in-maids or midwives. In reality, midwives were not among the preferred victims of prosecution (Haustein 1990, pp. 127, 177; Labovie 1991, pp. 180–1). Perhaps due to the high infant mortality rate, children were often seen as victims of a woman who had already been suspected of being a witch because of a superego conflict. Since the damage did not always follow the conflict immediately, it was easy to interpret the illness of a new-born child as harm caused by a witch. Roper constrains psychoanalysis with her belief in finding oedipal fantasies and the imago of the bad mother, which are indeed part of the imago of the witch, and which she believes to find in reality. Sexual threats and severe inner conflicts, which are warded off by sexualisation, become an oedipal fantasy. In Roper's study, Freud's seduction theory is interpreted one-sidedly in favour of oedipal fantasies. The complicated process of sexual abuse or sexualised and threatening situations leading oedipal fantasies in certain directions, deepening them and causing severe inner conflicts, which must be defended, is reduced to a wishful fantasy. Victims become offenders. In her opinion, the sexualised behaviour is no longer a product of abuse, threatening situations or sexual fears of a seductive oedipal object, especially in male development, but just the daughter's wishful fantasy. In Roper's study, the imago of the bad mother is not a fantasy of pursuit, which can be projected on to women, but real women who are supposed to be bad mothers. Roper explains: 'Here it is no coincidence that this period also saw a dramatic increase in executions of the ultimate evil mother, the woman who commits infanticide: such women had to be executed' (Roper 1994,

p. 217). Dülmen (1991), on the other hand, shows in his thorough historical study that the accusations against child-murderesses in the seventeenth century presumably increased, although infanticide did not; the pressure on women had risen. In my opinion, the imago of the witch also includes the imago of the bad mother and the oedipal seducer. This imago is first applied to women through processes of projective identification by complicated interactions, in which feelings of guilt play an important part. Women executed as witches were not really bad mothers or seductive young girls.

Psychoanalysis and culture

Psychological examination of historical phenomena has developed not only from educational theory, psychology or historical studies, but also from cultural sociology. The two volumes by Elias (1978, 1982) on the civilising process should be mentioned in particular. In these works, Elias explains how the civilising process is accompanied by an ever-increasing obligation to self-compulsion. In this point he totally agrees with Freud's theory of the evolution of man.

" In these and other elementary activities, the manner in which the individual behaves and feels slowly changes. This change is in the direction of a gradual 'civilization', but only historical experience makes clearer what this word actually means. It shows, for example, the decisive role played in this civilizing process by a very specific change in the feelings of shame and delicacy. The standard of what society demands and prohibits changes; in conjunction with this, the threshold of socially instilled displeasure and fear moves; and the question of sociogenic fears thus emerges as one of the central problems of the civilizing process.

" Very closely related to this is the further range of questions. The distance in behavior and whole psychical structure between children and adults increases in the course of the civilizing process. Here, for example, lies the key to the question of why some people or groups of people appear to us as 'younger' or 'more childlike', others as 'older' or 'more grown-up'. What we are trying to express in this way are differences in the kind and stage of the civilizing process that these societies have attained. (Elias 1978, pp. xii-xiii)

As far as the civilising process is concerned, Elias is very reminiscent of Freud, but he replaces heredity and the repetition compulsion with the interweaving of human impulses and strivings. Elias considers the interdependence of man and the interconnection of human plans and actions as a driving force for a historical change. These elements result in a structure which cannot be equated with the individual's will or reason. 'It is this order of interweaving human impulses and strivings, this social order, which determines the course of historical change; it underlies the civilizing process' (Elias 1982, p. 230).

The more closely knit the social interdependence within which the individual is bound, and the larger the area occupied by the society that the interdependence covers, the more spontaneous turmoil has to be mollified. Affects have to be repressed, violence has to be monopolised and isolated out and thoughts have to go beyond the moment (Elias 1982, p. 229–47).

Elias describes an important aspect of the development of the Occidental culture with the development of self-compulsion and the increasing suppression of affects and proves it with an impressive historical study of sources, which methodologically represents an important extension compared to Freud.

However, one cannot explain complicated psychic problems like the fear of witches or the possession in the sixteenth and seventeenth centuries simply with the development towards more self-compulsion.

Lloyd deMause (1974), a representative of psychohistory, frequently quoted in this study, also utilises a very narrow concept of evolution. He understands psychohistory as applied psychoanalysis and replaces Freud's concept of repetition compulsion with the concept of evolution.

> Since the repetition compulsion, by definition, cannot explain historical change, every attempt by Freud, Roheim, Kardiner and others to develop a theory of change ultimately ended in a sterile chicken-or-egg dispute about whether child-rearing depends on cultural traits or the other way around. That child-rearing practices are the basis for adult personality was proven again and again. Where they originated stumped every psychoanalyst who raised the question. (deMause 1974, p. 2)

As I tried to illustrate earlier, Freud did not consider repetition compulsion to be the motor of social development. DeMause here reduces Freud's theory and is only able to describe the changes of historical periods with a concept of evolution characterised by a belief in progress, which again is reminiscent of Freud.

DeMause refers to his approach as a psychogenetic theory of history. The central driving force of historical change is neither seen in technology nor economics, but in the psychogenetic changes in the personality or in the structure of the character which result from the interaction of parents and children throughout the generations. His theory is grounded on the following five basic assumptions which, according to deMause, can all be either verified or falsified by empirical and historical evidence:

- That evolution of parent–child relations constitutes an independent source of historical change. The origin of this evolution lies in the ability of successive generations of parents to regress to the psychic age of their children and work through the anxieties of that age in a better manner the second time they encounter them than they did during their own childhood.

- That this 'generational pressure' for psychic change is not only spontaneous, but also occurs independently of social and technological change.

- That the history of childhood is a series of closer approaches between adult and child, with each closing of psychic distance producing fresh anxiety. The reduction of this adult anxiety is the main source of the child-rearing practices of each age.

- The further back one goes in history, the less effective parents are in meeting the developing needs of the child.

- That because psychic structure must always be passed from generation to generation through the narrow funnel of childhood, a society's child-rearing practices are not just one item on a list of cultural traits. They are the very condition for the transmission and development of all other cultural elements, and place definite limits on what can be achieved in all other spheres of history. Specific childhood experiences must occur to sustain specific cultural traits, and once these experiences no longer occur the trait disappears. (deMause 1974, p. 3)

While I appreciate that deMause uses historical sources in order to support his psychogenetic theory in which he tries to include actual cultural development, he unfortunately fails to acknowledge the interrelation between cultural and psychic development. Historical phenomena only serve as verifications or falsifications of his psychogenetic theory. He explicitly declares that the evolution of the parent–child relationship is an independent source for historical change. Psychic change occurs independently from social and technological change. From my perspective, it does not seem very likely that the parents' ability to go back to the psychic age of a child and thus better understand their children's anxieties, could constitute the driving force for psychological change in history.

DeMause perceives evolution as a continuous development, a development in the course of which parents become increasingly able to understand their children. This striking deficiency in deMause's theory is revealed when the theory is applied to Early Modern times. If psychic change can be explained by improvement in childhood conditions, how is it possible that, during the witch persecutions, childhood conditions did not undergo a similar positive development but rather the contrary? Can the sending-away of the children in the era of ambivalence, as deMause characterises the Early Modern times, in fact be traced back to a better understanding of the parents of former generations? Is it possible to come to an understanding of culture by considering child-rearing practices alone? Should we not instead understand these practices as having a psychodynamic function of supporting adaption to the respective society?

In order to understand the relation between psychic development and culture, one has to again turn to ethnology – in particular to ethno-psychoanalysis. Ethno-psychoanalysis examines the individual's conscious and unconscious conflicts within the respective culture. The foreign culture is not regarded as more mature or more highly developed than another culture, and the tendency inherent in the concept of evolution to degrade previous generations is not adopted. Unconscious conflicts caused by culture are regarded as functional for this particular culture, that is, as an unconscious process of adaptation.

Devereux, the founder of ethno-psychoanalysis, carried out his research mainly among the Sedang Moi in Vietnam and the Native American Mohave in the US. He presumes the existence of an unconscious composed of two elements – the ethnic and the idiosyncratic. The individual's ethnic unconscious is that part of his entire unconscious which he or she shares with the majority of his or her cultural peers. It is composed of all the concepts that one generation forces the next to repress, meeting the fundamental requirements of that particular generation. Just like the culture, this ethnic unconscious is subject to transformation and is passed on not biologically, but through some sort of instruction. The ethnic unconscious is acquired through interaction with the particular culture.

According to Devereux, each culture allows certain kinds of fantasies, drives and other manifestations of the psyche to enter and to dwell on the conscious level, while others require repression. This is the reason why all members of the same culture share a certain number of unconscious conflicts. However, the defence mechanisms offered to the individual by his or her culture in order to repress his or her culturally dystonic drives can prove insufficient. In this case, many individuals – and not only those who suffered from atypical early childhood traumata – struggle to master and conceal their conflicts (Devereux 1982, p. 12).

Devereux points out that the idiosyncratic unconscious is composed of elements resulting from the individual's compulsion to repress them because of unique and specific burdens he or she has had to carry. The idiosyncratic traumata evoke conflicts within the individual, which permanently remain within the private or individual unconscious (Devereux 1982, pp. 11–16).

Culture assists the ethnic unconscious in its defence process. Between outer and inner reality, the substance of myths, belief and attitudes form a medium level, which receives special attention. According to Devereux, this material in some respect represents a defence mechanism, since it offers a kind of 'refrigerator' where fantasies resulting from inner conflicts can be stored. Ethnopsychoanalysis takes a look into the unconscious dynamics of culture and individual. Culture influences the process of an individual's repression and at the same time it offers defence mechanisms. In this way, members of one culture are bound to it affectively. From this point of view, unconscious conflicts have a central function within the cultural adaptation process. The key to an exploration of unconscious dynamics within one culture is to be found within ethno-psychoanalytic methods.

Freud maintained: 'But I have had good reason for asserting that everyone possesses in his own unconscious an instrument with which he can interpret the utterances of the unconscious in other people' (Freud 1913, p. 320). Devereux points out that ethno-psychoanalysis includes self-reflection by the researcher, deep emotional involvement with other people and reflection on one's own emotional reactions in an unfamiliar culture. Without these features, cognition is impossible. According to him, the interpretation of transference is less revolutionary in psychoanalysis than analysing counter-transference because the information gained from transference could also be obtained from other sources. If, however, the researcher's traditional attitudes are questioned when he is confronted with the unfamiliar, leading him to reject the new experience, counter-transference acts as a means of defence and prevents cognition. According to Devereux, this is the origin of behavioural sciences.

" In short, behavioral science data arouse anxieties, which are warded off by a countertransference inspired pseudo-methodology; this maneuver is responsible for nearly all the defects of behavioral science. (Devereux 1967, p. xvii)

Unknown social conditions and other factors cause anxieties and uncertainties. If applied carefully and consciously, the counter-transference reaction can be seen as an important research method, a way of understanding the unknown, though only as one way among many. Ethno-psychoanalyis has a very important advantage, and that is that cultures can be directly experienced through confrontation. Ethno-psychoanalysis benefits from the opportunity of communicating with members of foreign cultures so that transference and counter-transference reactions may be fully experienced and reflected. In this respect, ethno-psychoanalysis can enter into real relationships.

In the field of history, however, this is not possible, as it a discipline which in most cases is restricted to meagre sources that often do not provide sufficient information from which to draw psychoanalytic conclusions. All too often, psychoanalysts have to rely on secondary sources, whereas historians often have to content themselves with psychoanalytic findings drawn from books. As a consequence, transference reactions that also originate from historical sources cannot be properly transmitted.

How can we succeed in better understanding the specific relations between the inner conflicts in the ethnic unconscious, their defence and their function in the process of adapting to the respective culture?

Parin, Morgenthaler and Parin-Matthèy (1963, 1978) assume that basic ideas taken from psychoanalysis can be employed to understand a foreign culture, but they warn of applying our concepts of normalcy and abnormality to other cultures (Heinrichs 1982, p. 63). While studying the behaviour of the Dogon and Agni in West Africa, Parin discovered that, 'the oedipal formula, that is, the desire to possess the mother and to kill the father, is already a culture-specific concept ... In the Dogon culture, the paternal rival figure is distributed and then disposed of through mutual identifications, and not through introjection of that figure's attitude of rejection (Parin 1973, p. 245).

Besides the defence of drive conflicts, Parin examines the importance of so-called adaption mechanisms. Parin regards the group ego and the clan conscience as adaption mechanisms which 'relieve the ego of any confrontation with the outside world, comparable to the way in which the defence mechanisms (according to Anna Freud's theories) do so with respect to the rejected instinctive needs' (Parin et al. 1978, p. 82).

The term, 'group ego' defines the identificational interaction as follows:

" We attribute the development of the group ego to identificational relationships which are relatively free of tension and which are established during childhood or adolescence between individuals of equal age and sex in 'horizontal groups'. If there are communities or groups in a social situation in which, because of their structures, and the particular psychology of their members, mutual brotherly and sisterly identification is possible, the group ego is a guarantee for good social adaption (e.g. in the Dogon village). This adaptation mechanism mirrors the community structure of a society more precisely than others. In a nuclear family, there is no room for this mechanism. In the public life of an urbanised industrial society it must fail. (Parin et al. 1978, p. 87)

Parin, Morgenthaler and Parin-Matthèy describe the clan conscience as a kind of external superego: 'The Dogon have not internalised the images of parental figures, with their demand that certain drives be rejected, as permanently as we have. Instead of warding off their drives, they have replaced the figures of their early childhood, split up their meaning and transferred it to people in the environment during adulthood' (Parin et al. 1963, p. 500).

The clan conscience relieves the ego of unbearable anxieties, feelings of guilt or their archaic forerunners. This leads to a sort of identification with the role which restricts the mobility of the ego. The ego is able to retain the capability to replace the internalised superego temporarily with external authorities or institutions. They are supplied with the same drive energies and have prohibitive and rewarding effects on the ego. The clan conscience is restricted in that it loses all independence with respect to its social surroundings which, after overcoming shame and guilt *vis-à-vis* the internalised superego, it can then enjoy.

" The term adaption mechanism refers to mechanisms which are more or less firmly established in the ego of an adult, and which function unconsciously, automatically and identically to the way that has been described with respect to defence mechanisms. While these defence mechanisms have established themselves within the ego to ward off unwanted or disturbing drives, desires or affects, the purpose of the adaption mechanisms we are referring to, is to cope with the influences of the social environment. (Parin 1977, p. 481)

According to Parin, adaption mechanisms do not have the function of defending one's drives. These mechanisms should meet the demands of the environment and thus provide relative stability for the ego. 'The fact that this ego shows a defence organisation which permits the stimulation of the drives should continue to be seen in relation to the psychic reality of fantasies, desires and anxieties, rather than to the environment and its influences' (Parin 1977, p. 488).

In Parin's opinion, there is no permanent connection between adaption mechanisms and affect. If these mechanisms work properly, Parin continues, the result will be well-being, whereas the failure to adjust will lead to anxiety.

Defence mechanisms require energy (counter-cathexis) to free the ego from its libidinal desires, whereas adaption mechanisms relieve the ego of this task. While one could regard the defence mechanisms as an expression of conflictive drives rooted in one's childhood (or as the heritage built up in the ego), the adaption mechanisms are a more obvious indicator of how the social environment influences the structure of the ego: they are also established during childhood, but are constantly subject to social forces.

In this model, outward adaption occurs automatically; identification always offers satisfaction and narcissistic gain, and strengthens one's identity. Here, Parin's orientation to ego-psychology is clear in that adaption to a norm expected by the social surroundings is understood, whereby those elements producing conflicts in the adaption process are lost. According to Parin, the group ego derives from conflict-free identification relationships. Are there conflict-free spheres in the process of adaption? Can adaption mechanisms be regarded separately from defence mechanisms?

If we consider the results of my case study of the matrilineal culture in Palau (Heinemann 1995), we can see that the educational methods lead to a high degree of oral satisfaction of drives. The mother is relieved of all work for up to ten months after the birth of the child and is supplied with delicacies by her brothers and her husband.

The infant is to be fed whenever it is hungry. As a rule, it is abruptly separated from the mother at ten months and from then onwards is also looked after by other female members of the clan. In my opinion, this abrupt separation leads to a deep and lifelong separation-anxiety, which remains in the ethnic unconscious. This anxiety is further intensified by adoption. About a third of the children are adopted within the mother's, or less frequently the father's, clan. During my stay in Palau this fear became tangible, as I was asked almost daily whether I was really going to stay there for some time or leave the next day.

The educational practices generate unconscious conflicts for which the culture, as Devereux understands it, provides a means of defence. Identification with a group of people of the same age and sex with which the member of the clan is connected for his lifetime, supports the defence of drives. The anxiety of being abandoned by the mother produces an anxiety of being expelled from the group. The adoption of the group's rules is unconsciously guaranteed because it serves to ward off the separation anxiety. A tradition of physical and individual punishment does not exist in Palau culture. Adaption to cultural demands is realised through the culture's creation of these conflicts in education for which it later supplies adequate defence mechanisms in the form of rites and social institutions. Adaption mechanisms are provided by society in a way, that they support the defence of drives or of narcissistic conflicts. If cultural demands change, educational practices have to change as well. This raises new demands with respect to the conflicts existing in the ethnic unconscious. Will this understanding of defence and adaption mechanisms help us to better understand the phenomenon of the Early Modern Age?

7 The Study in the Light of Psychoanalytic Theory

Witches, Saints and the Superego

If we consider the historical development from the thirteenth to the fifteenth centuries, we can see an increase in the number of female saints who considered themselves to be the bride of Jesus. They lived ascetically, rejected food and sometimes exhibited self-destructive behaviour. Did these women offer a means of defence (Devereux) in which typical conflicts of the ethnic unconscious could be stored and worked out? The notions of the witch that replaced that of saintliness starting in the fifteenth and sixteenth centuries appear as reversals into the opposite. What psychic alterations were expressed in this change? Did the psychic structure and the inner conflicts of the people of that time change? Did any changes take place toward adaption to society and the defence of drive conflicts?

Chasseguet-Smirgel (1987, pp. 20–1) considers the image of the virgin birth as a means to avoid the Oedipus complex. The idea that the mother becomes pregnant without penetration and that it is the birth which deflowers the mother expresses the accomplice character of the child with the oedipally seductive mother. The father does nothing which the child could not do either with its pre-genital sexuality. The birth of Jesus gives the son a more genital role than that of his father because the son deflowers the mother during birth. Pre-genital sexuality is subject to an idealisation process. This would mean that in pre-Reformation times, adaption to culture was not achieved through the classical Oedipus complex, but by the avoidance of the oedipal situation.

The analysis of the painter Christoph Haitzmann by Freud (1923b) reveals that the notion of being saved by the Virgin Mary helps to prevent oedipal desires during a boy's development into manhood. The relationship to the mother is not resolved through triangulation and oedipal conflicts. The disidentification with the mother in order to gain male identity (Greenson 1968) is not possible through the boy's identification with the father. The mother remains incestuously seductive and threatening. Oedipal fantasies are warded off by the ascetic attitude, the denial of genital sexuality and self-punishment. The superego is mainly shaped by pre-genital conflicts and remains externalised. The ego submits to Mary and Jesus, who in turn promise to supply the painter, Haitzmann, with food (oral satisfaction) in the cave in the desert.

Jones (1972) considers the emergence of the Reformation as a transition from a negative to a positive oedipal complex. According to Jones, the Catholic attitude towards God was characterised by subjugation during the years prior to the Reformation. People tried to obtain the love of God by a feminine attitude towards him. Feminisation and symbolic castration are expressed by celibacy, the priest's robe and his tonsure. The feminine attitude results in an extremely intense castration anxiety, which, according to Jones, is revealed for example in the belief in the Immaculate Conception of the Virgin Mary. The identification with the Virgin facilitated the feminine attitude. The devotion to her, however, came to an end when the Reformation began.

Protestant clergymen were allowed to marry. They had overcome their feminine attitude towards God. Jones traces this change in the attitude towards God back to a new stage of oedipal development.

" One could say that the Protestant solution of the Oedipal complex lies in replacing the mother with the wife, whereas the Catholic solution lies in turning the male role into the female role. (Jones 1972, p. 211)

Is it possible that this change in the oedipal development was initiated by the women who, despite living in asceticism, desired to be Christ's bride? Has it thus become impossible to deny oedipal fantasies and has the fear of witches been derived from an anxiety of punishment for these impulses?

During my field research on fakafefines in Tonga, Polynesia (Heinemann 1998), I myself was able to experience the oedipal situation of young men, who are tied to their mother in a highly incestuous relationship, because they are not allowed to turn to their fathers or any group of men. Fakafefines are men who, from their very childhood, stay in an extremely close relationship to their mothers. They are raised as girls and are not allowed to go to work with the men. They continue to sleep in the same room as their sisters; this is forbidden for 'male' brothers once they have reached the age of six. To protect themselves against this incestuous bond with their mothers or sisters, fakafefines deny their sex.

The development of transvestite and transsexual behaviour serves as a defence against oedipal anxiety (of an incestuous relationship with the mother) and pre-oedipal anxiety (of becoming one with the mother). The focus on brother–sister incest, a complex which, analogous to the oedipal complex in our culture, is an adaption to a society in which it is not a father and a mother, but a brother and a sister who represent the leaders of the clan and society.

During a conversation I had in Tonga, this threatening incestuous relationship with the mother occurred. I wanted to talk to one of these young fakafefines about his childhood and youth, which really scared him. He sought help, calling for another young man, who was standing with a group of other men not far away from us. The young man came over and the fakafefine I had addressed initially said that I should talk to his friend first, as he had also been brought up as a girl during childhood.

He said that he would like to listen to the conversation first. After talking with the two young men about their life stories and the development of their feelings for a while, a strong affect emerged in the transference. The young man I had talked to first asked me if I could arrange a date between him and the young German woman who was staying at the same hotel as I was. His affect became increasingly urgent: 'She is so beautiful. I really would like to meet her.' He had the idea of writing her a letter and asked me for paper. Having finished the letter, he asked the other young man to take the letter to the hotel and to slide it under the door of the young German's room. In a state of extreme excitement he said that she would certainly meet him that day already. Now the other young man asked which was the door to the young German woman's room. The first young man said: 'Watch out that you don't slide it under the wrong door!' When he said this, his affect of longing turned into anxiety and he said: 'Imagine if you slid the letter under the old woman's door!' Then both young men went to the hotel.

In the transference, the oedipal striving manifested itself in the form of the seductive young German woman, which then turned into anxiety when the fantasy was fulfilled (when the letter was slid under the door). The seductive young woman turned into the old woman who was travelling alone and who was staying at the hotel, too. I had also noticed her because of her advanced age and because of the fact that she was still travelling alone at that age. Since I was German and was also travelling alone, the fantasy contained aspects of myself. The libidinal desire (the young woman) and the anxiety of incest (the overwhelming old woman) were warded off by splitting and reversal into the opposite. In the young man's imagination, the old woman who was travelling alone turned into a witch with threatening aspects of an incestuous oedipal relation with his mother. In the male development in particular, the fear of witches is an expression of a man's pre-genital relationship with his mother, a relationship lacking a father or a group of men that are necessary for the individuation and integration of genital impulses.

In Collomb's opinion (1978), there is a close relation between the African tales of witchcraft and cannibalism, mythical witch reports and the mother–son relationship of early childhood. The conflict, which consists in separation from one's mother and in building up sexual relations, is dealt with in the witch fantasies. Collomb tells the story of a mythical healer called Bandia Waly, an independent son who killed his mother just as she tried to kill him. This story comes from Senegal. Bandia Waly's nine brothers wanted to marry nine young girls living in the west. The mother of the young man was pregnant and shortly after the departure of her nine sons, the child in her womb demanded to be born. Bandia Waly set off to catch up with his brothers, but since they did not want Bandia Waly to accompany them, they almost beat him to death. Only when he revealed himself as their youngest brother did they accept his company. When they finally arrived at the house of the brides, their mother staked a claim to Bandia Waly, arguing that he was her bridegroom. She wanted to spend the night with him, while the nine brothers went to bed with the nine brides. Bandia Waly replaced the blankets of his brothers with those of the brides. At night, the old witch crept into the bedroom of the brothers and cut the throats of the nine young women in the conviction that she was killing the brothers. Bandia Waly woke up his brothers and they all ran away. But the old witch chased them and eventually managed to catch up with them. As she tried to push Bandia Waly into the fire, he jumped aside and instead pushed the witch into the fire. According to Collomb, this story is about murder in two respects: a mother murdering her child and a child murdering his mother. Bandia Waly kills the witch who is his mother as well as his bride.

According to Collomb (1978, p. 478) the way people accused of witchcraft are treated in Senegal differs from the way they were treated in Europe in Early Modern Times. In Senegal, the accused are reintegrated into society after they have made a confession. Using his knowledge and autonomy, Bandia Waly manages to release himself from the traditional mother–son relationship. This act of liberating oneself from such a traditional dyadic relationship is a psychic complex as is the oedipal complex which expresses a tripartite relationship. 'Every African can identify with Bandia Waly but has difficulty identifying with Oedipus', Collomb says (1978, p. 481).

Cannibalistic aggression contributes to the gaining of separation and individuation from the mother–child relationship, a process which is particularly endangered in the male's development towards maturity. For boys, in contrast to girls, the oral and oedipal objects are equivalents. On the island of Tonga, only men are allowed to participate in the so-called Kava ceremony, a repeated ritual in the course of which they symbolically eat their mothers and sisters (Heinemann 1998, pp. 476–9). This cannibalistic aggression is essential for the separation from the mother and admission to the group of adult men. In the pre-Reformation era, the development of this aggression is both suppressed and avoided in the public concept of virginity. The threat caused by incest is denied in the image of asceticism. The anxiety of witchcraft was bound to emerge when the Virgin Mary no longer served as a symbol of adaption to the prevailing culture, as was the case in the sixteenth century. The predominance of young men as victims of witches shows that the fear of witches derives from an incestuous mother image which is especially anxietyed during male development.

Demos (1982, pp. 156–7) considers the lasting dependency of men on their mothers to be the primary reason for the fear of witches in seventeenth-century New England. The marriageable age for men was 25, and youth lasted until the age of 30.

" Young men supplied a far larger number of victims than any other category. Moreover, their sense of liability to attack can be interpreted as expressing several convergent strands of inner concern with women of their mothers' generation. In the first place, the witch commands extraordinary power over them and their possessions. (They continue to feel the strengths of the 'maternal object.') At the same time, they strike postures of resistance and repudiation – refusing the witch's request for co-operation in routine aspects of everyday experience, and leading the charge against her in the courts of law. (They wish, however they can, to break the 'incestuous' tie.) For this the witch grows angry with them, and punishes them severely. (They feel guilty, and deserving of punishment, for what they are about.) But when the witch attacks them, she does so indirectly, i.e. through familiars, or by striking down their cattle. (Distance is still maintained; in fantasy, as in social reality, the 'maternal object' must not come to close.) (Demos 1982, p. 157)

The witch trials in New England investigated by Demos involved 76 male and 57 female victims. Most of the men were between 20 and 40, the second largest group were elderly women, and the third largest group of the victims were young girls (Demos 1982, p. 154). The image of the Virgin Mary served mainly as a means of warding off men's incestuous anxiety during male development. Nevertheless, young women also anxietyed the aggression of their oedipal mothers when they did not obey them like, for instance, Nicole Obri, who indulged in dancing and pleasure, or Anna Tschudi, who showed her aggression openly. Although female saints between the thirteenth and fifteenth centuries, by living ascetically, supported their ability to adapt to a development in which oedipal conflicts were increasingly avoided, they also insisted on the oedipal fantasy of being Christ's bride.

According to Weinstein and Bell (1982), as well as Bell (1985), the 'age of the saints' lasted from 1200 to 1500. In the sixteenth and seventeenth centuries, the number of saints decreased dramatically (Weinstein and Bell 1982, p. 45). In the eleventh and twelfth centuries, saints were found mainly among the nobility, but in the thirteenth century, the number of saints among the lower classes also increased. Until the thirteenth century, saints were usually male. In the thirteenth century, three out of four saints were male (p. 224).

During the period from the fourteenth century until the Reformation, the number of female saints in the monasteries declined, whereas the number of women among the population who considered themselves to be saints increased. In the fourteenth and fifteenth centuries, half of all female saints in Italy had never been nuns. The adoration of female saints reached its peak around the year 1500 (Bell 1985, pp. 149–50).

Weinstein and Bell (1982) and Bell (1985) thought of the female saints merely as adolescent girls who preferred the autonomy provided by monasteries to sexuality and marriage to an unwanted man. The authors describe the saints as holy anorexics, because their behaviour already bore symptoms of the disorder today known as anorexia. Weinstein and Bell find themselves faced with the problem of projecting modern syndromes on to past times.

" Between the ages of four and seven, occasionally a bit later, a medieval girl began to be aware of what society had in store for her. From her peers, from the church, but most especially from her parents, she learned the norms of her class and sex. She might be allowed a few more years of frivolous play, but already she was being subtly cued for courtship, marriage and motherhood. (Weinstein and Bell 1982, p. 42)

For young girls, the sight of white-clad nuns in the streets was very appealing. Religious identification with the Virgin Mary offered considerable comfort. The girls found themselves trapped in a conflict between the flesh and the spiritual world.

" Invariably the conflict escalated: against the parents' greater worldly strength the child needed greater spiritual resources, resources sought in ever greater spiritual extremes of self-mortification. (Weinstein and Bell 1982, p. 44)

In 48 per cent of all cases mentioned in Weinstein and Bell (1982, p. 71), the decision to take up a religious calling was made during adolescence. The reactions of parents and society to this decision varied from century to century. The motivations for the decision to enter the state of holiness were a desire for chastity in the fight against the temptations of the flesh and the conflict brought about by parents pressing for an unwanted marriage. Margaret, for example, threatened to cut off her nose and lips should she be forced to marry. Consequently, nobody bothered her (Weinstein and Bell 1982, p. 88).

Girls had to marry the men chosen by their fathers. There was hardly any support or sympathy to be expected from the parents. Identification with the Virgin Mary offered an opportunity to escape from the demands of marriage and motherhood. The most important female saints were virgins.

If they turned to religion during adulthood, this was usually a reaction to a crisis and to conflicts like the death of a beloved person, a serious illness, supernatural experiences, or sudden guilt feelings of guilt for the sins committed in their past (Weinstein and Bell 1982, pp. 98–101). Most of the saints were virgins or widows (Weinstein and Bell 1982, p. 87).

Bell (1985, p. 56) describes the inner struggle of the saintly girls. They were superstitious, strong-willed girls. As children, they were often raised by strictly religious mothers, and forced to marry early by their fathers. They offered resistance, developed anorexic symptoms and sought refuge in the convent. Their fathers either relented or eventually died. Later on, the girls were tormented by demons and were incapable of eating. Some of them recovered in their early thirties and joined convents. As nuns they then fasted voluntarily.

Others did not recover, but tortured themselves with aggressive self-destruction. They whipped and burnt themselves to exorcise their inner demons (Bell 1985, p. 112). These women identified themselves with the suffering of Christ. In their bodies, they carried the original sin, the responsibility for the Saviour's death. This is what Bell calls ascetic masochism of the saintly anorexic virgins (p. 113).

Half of the 42 Italians of the thirteenth century who have been recognised as saints supposedly showed anorexic behaviour. According to Bell (1985, p. 149), a new ideal of saintliness emerged. Young women were looking for autonomy and rejected Mary's passive, reproductive role. They struggled against their demons by means of ever-increasing torture, and denied hunger and weariness. Later on, they became incapable of eating or sleeping. Their sexual needs were fulfilled by their idea of a mystic unity with God. They only hungered for the host, for the body of their 'husband'. In the late fifteenth century, the mediaeval model was called into question and considered the work of the Devil. A hundred years earlier, everyone would have recognised the voice of God as such, now they believed that the Devil had spoken (Bell 1985, p. 157) (see Chapter 5).

I do agree with Bell (1985) that the unconscious meaning of the refusal to eat practised both by the saints of the fourteenth and fifteenth centuries and by the anorexic girls of today is to be found in the equating of food with sexuality. Not eating means having no sexuality. On the other hand, considering saints to be anorexic persons who resolved their struggle for autonomy by entering the convent is, in my opinion, a projection of the modern image of anorexia on to history. Life in the convent is thus unrealistically idealised as promoting autonomy. After all, the lives of the male or female saints, like the medical history of the painter Haitzmann, show that monastery or convent life catered to the desire for punishment and masochistic forms of defence.

Habermas (1990, pp. 46–8) emphasises that saints solved their adolescence conflicts by asserting themselves against their fathers and the ecclesiastical authorities by entering a convent. He says that, in contrast, anorexic girls of today are afraid of autonomy and therefore could not break away from their families. According to Habermas, equating those two manifestations on the basis of parallel symptoms suggests a neglect of the cultural context. Nevertheless, he also emphasises the autonomy conflict in both manifestations. If we assume that psychic development and structure in the fourteenth and fifteenth centuries were different from those of our times, we cannot call the saints anorexic, even if the adolescence conflicts of that time and today are similar.

Adolescence as a phase of development always means dealing with the integration of sexuality and exogamy, which, however, can be achieved in different ways. Adolescence is regarded as the last phase of solving oedipal conflicts, of breaking away from the family as well as establishing the superego. This helps to solve oedipal conflicts as well as the ambivalence conflicts associated with them (Jacobson 1973, p. 183).

The contemplation of childhood in the Early Modern Age (Chapter 3) shows us that drive conflicts and narcissistic conflicts cannot be compared to today's development. Oral and anal development presumably resulted in a drive-conflict that warded off a great deal of pre-genital aggression by submitting to external authorities (parents and the Church). Evil spirits (the projected aggression) had to be kept in check through the use of protective magic. The conflict was thus externalised. The avoidance of oedipal conflicts was also reflected in early childhood by the fact that children were sent to foster-parents while still very young and were given the status of grown-ups at the age of six, which could be seen by the manner in which they were dressed.

Turning to saints once more, we see that the aspects of defence, asceticism and self-punishment are prominent. Could it be that what is defended is, in fact, the more important element in those saintly women who indulged in their fantasies as brides of Christ? Were they not expressing the desire for oedipal and genital fulfilment while at the same time suppressing their desires through ascetic self-castigation? In contrast to possessed women, they punished themselves and also exorcised the Devil themselves. They were still victors in the struggle against the Devil, something that was still possible in the time before the sixteenth century. As brides of Christ, the women insisted on a relationship which, however, had to be asexual. They identified themselves not with the Virgin Mary but with Christ. The drive was warded off; the object however was already oedipal to some extent, but was being assimilated orally by identification or introjection.

Assuming that the idea of pre-genital sexuality in the image of the Virgin Mary represented a constraint upon women to submit themselves to their husbands' anxieties, the female saints basically insisted on oedipal development, that is, on the object of one's love. Wurmser (1998) describes masochism as the repeated attempt to reject loss and pain. 'The pain caused by suffering protects you from the even greater pain caused by a loss' (Wurmser 1998, p. 91). The masochist overemphasises the importance of the object relation and denies the significance of discharging one's drives: Do not rival anyone but sacrifice yourself, do not hurt and kill but heal, do not feel anger but grief, do not take murderous revenge on anyone but sacrifice something. Passiveness instead of self-assertion, surrender instead of competition, magical power instead of helplessness are the masochistic forms of defence (p. 147). As the saints sought an oedipal object, the anxiety of the threatening aspect of the drive grew, as did the anxiety of the imago of the witch and the Devil. This resulted in possession and the fear of witches as well as in a growing internalisation and autonomy of the superego.

The case of the painter Haitzmann and the saints reveals dynamics of temptation by the Devil, as well as a complete reversal into the opposite of the libidinal desire – the Devil is seen as a threat and has to be defeated. The Devil appears in visions and the saints gain their power through asceticism. The price they had to pay was surrender, and the female saints, unlike the painter, retained the oedipal object since they were convinced that they were the brides of Christ. The women were obliged to react even more strongly with self-castigation. The female saints punished the drive, while the object was retained and incorporated orally. The painter Haitzmann, however, surrendered to the motherly Virgin and hoped for an oral reward for giving up his oedipal desires.

The possessed person is seen to increasingly repress and relegate the conflict to the unconscious. Temporarily, the Devil gains control – sometimes he represents the punishing superego, sometimes the impulse of the drive. The externalised superego was appeased by submission to external authorities. With the increasing internalisation of some aspects of the superego, the Devil also inflicted punishment, for example, when he made Nicole Obri (Chapter 5) fall down the cellar stairs. Thus it was no longer the possessed who punished themselves; this role was taken over by internalised parts of the superego instead. Perhaps it was precisely these strong oral aggressions that added fuel to the fear of witches and drove women to search for an oedipal object. Modern therapies show that oral aggression can have a strong influence on oedipal development.

" In both sexes excessive development of pre-genital, especially oral aggression tends to induce a premature development of Oedipal strivings, and as a consequence a particular pathological condensation between pre-genital and genital aims under the overriding influence of aggressive needs. (Kernberg 1975, p. 43)

" Severe oral pathology tends to develop the positive Oedipal strivings prematurely in the girl. Genital strivings for the father are used as a substitute gratification of oral-dependent needs that have been frustrated by the dangerous mother. Strong unconscious guilt feelings exist about Oedipal strivings. The idealised mother image is completely split off from the dangerous, threatening mother image. The efforts to obtain gratification from idealised partial mother figures tend to fail because of ever-present oral-aggressive needs and anxiety. (Kernberg 1975, p. 42)

The dependency on an externalised superego that supposedly existed before the era of the witch persecutions did not only lead to an avoidance of oedipal anxieties, but also to submission to external authorities. Whether this has always taken place in form of subjugation to precursors of the sadistic superego as is known in today's treatment of patients (Klein 1972, Jacobson 1973, Kernberg 1975) is doubtful in a historical sense. The mediaeval attitude towards handicapped children, the belief in contact with demons who replaced normal human children, shows that these demons were not only considered to be sadistic, but also that one could negotiate with them. At least the idea of mediaeval changelings led to the partial acceptance of the handicapped. Mothers had no feelings of guilt and were able to deal with their children without being overprotective – a reaction formation against strong aggression.

The moral obligation and practice of mutual aid, which, out of anxiety of punishment and in the hope of a reward in the hereafter made people act in a benevolent manner (Schindler 1992, p. 265), shows that non-oedipal forms of the superego do not by any means have to be merely sadistic, and that they can possibly have a morally higher standard than the oedipal superego. The superego based on internalisation also leads to the turning of aggression against oneself. Once re-projected, it can release considerable aggression.

According to Parin (1973), the so-called clan conscience works in such a way that authorities from the outside world embody the conscience. Powerful leaders, healers and magicians threaten the individual with lethal punishment. This is an introjection of a raping maternal phallus, from which the person takes the strength to act in accordance with moral constraints. Without such identification and dominant forms, the appearance of which sometimes derives from the father, but whose function always derives from the mother starting in early childhood, orientation is lost (Parin 1973, p. 244).

In the matrilineal culture of Palau (Heinemann 1995) the externalised superego imagines, that is, the totemistic gods, draw attention to offences and are responsible for ensuring that social rules are obeyed. The gods have to be satisfied. Yet they are benevolent and rewarding, and offer possibilities for reparations if rules are violated. Physical punishment is unknown in traditional education. The superego is the collective superego with high moral standards and cannot be equated with sadistic types of the superego.

Ethno-psychoanalytic research shows that an externalised maternal superego type as well as an oedipal one can develop different degrees and levels of maturity. They are not sadistic precursors of the superego, but depend on the development of narcissistic and libidinal conflicts, that is, socialisation and education.

Grunberger's (1974) theory of the maternal superego is also a result of therapy studies and therefore draws different conclusions than those drawn by ethno-psychoanalytic studies. According to Grunberger, the early superego is a result of various introjections and identifications. It has deep pre-genital and narcissistic origins.

" Although it seems paradoxical at first, the moral superego, the conscience, has an eminent social aspect which applies even more to the early than to the Oedipal super-ego. Indeed, the early superego plays an important role in the religious, political, moral and social life of the individual. To a certain extent it determines the use of ideologies which are mainly of a superego character as we see from our daily experience. (Grunberger 1974, p. 509)

According to Grunberger, the superego in its early form is predominantly a collective phenomenon. It entails the necessity of adapting to the collective superego. Thus, it is undoubtedly an essential part of the collective phenomena. According to Grunberger, the primitive ego will submit to the superego and identify with it.

" It is useful here to recall the fact that the little crying child trapped in a relationship dominated by violence feels helpless in the face of the giant mother, who is terrifying, seen as the bearer of the child's projected aggression. She imposes her will on it without giving it the least possibility of resistance. By obeying her, the child assimilates precisely this absolute power and thus becomes the holder of the maternal omnipotence ... Having submitted to the mother's super-ego, there is no longer any need for the child to anxiety its own aggressiveness in the form of a corresponding retaliation. This is why the terrifying object becomes a trustworthy person. (Grunberger 1974, p. 515)

No one can be blamed as long as he or she follows the instructions of his or her mother because it is the anal maternal superego which mirrors the early training (Grunberger 1974, p. 521).

Total subjection is unquestioning, that is to say, there is no other arrangement to serve as a place of refuge. One obeys without knowing why, no other agreement or compromise being permitted. Actually, the baby does not have a choice: it has to obey its mother. The only thing it can do is to share the power with her.

According to Grunberger, the cannibalistic aggression of the baby nurtures the early superego of the baby, which demands blind obedience. On the other hand, however, it demands unconditional obedience and therefore reminds us of the initial mother–child relationship, which is both the origin and cause of cannibalistic aggression. The inexplicable is very powerful. It forces people to depend completely on the original mother and to identify themselves with her. The maternal superego acts as an opponent of the paternal. We are either subjected to the dictates of the collective or to our own conscience. The maternal superego results from a double identification, which consists, on the one hand, of identification with sadistic affects projected on the mother and thus with the same, reintrojected affects, and, on the other hand, with the results of training, although in a slightly altered form. It consists of ban taboos, that is, moral judgements in projected form. In Grunberger's view, this ban on the maternal superego acts as a weapon against the paternal superego as well as against the paternal world as a whole, and as a way of protecting oneself against all oedipal conflict situations (in order to avoid the Oedipus conflict).

The maternal superego only works in connection with clearly defined objects, with texts, regulations or dogmas. It is, according to Grunberger, obsessive, sadistic and unmerciful. The paternal superego is said to have a sense of reality and to be more flexible. The early superego leads to murder and projection, whereas the paternal superego is an inner support and seeks to achieve narcissistic perfection in the realisation of the ideals of life. The superego integrates narcissism and the drives, whereas the early superego is the cathexis of only the sadistic affects.

This notion of the superego has to be put into perspective from a historical and ethnological point of view. It was only with the establishment of an individual superego that the witch as an aggressive superego imago turned into a threatening, pursuing imago at the beginning of the Early Modern Age. The demons and Devils of the Middle Ages could be controlled by defensive spells, preventive magic and rituals.

Possessed Women and Hysteria

The symptoms shown by possessed women and hysterical women as described by Freud in his time are very similar to each other, even though we cannot treat these two phenomena as one because of different cultural circumstances. How, then, do we see hysteria today?

Classic hysteria distinguishes between symptoms of conversion and psychic functional disorders in the form of dissociative symptoms. Symptoms of conversion are: visual defects, difficulties in breathing, attacks of giddiness caused by psychic disorders, weakness of the muscles, paralysis, anaesthesia, hearing defects, language disorders and difficulties in swallowing, vomiting, trembling, not being able to stand upright, hysterical attacks accompanied by bending the trunk forwards and arching it backwards (arc de cercle), rhythmical cramped movements and coughing fits. Dissociative symptoms include states of semi-conciousness, memory black-outs as well as splits in the ego (Mentzos 1980, pp. 14–17).

This division was separated in DSM III (Diagnostic and Statistical Manual) and the hysterical neurosis was split; finally, in the later development of DSM III R, DSM IV and ICD 10 (International Classification of Diseases), hysteria was completely dissolved.

Mentzos (1996) advocates maintaining the diagnosis of hysteria, but to speak of it as the hysterical mode. According to the structure and maturity of the ego, this mode can be applied from psychosis to borderline disorder via neurosis to non-neurotic behaviour.

The aim of the hysterical mode is always an apparent change of self-representation. With regard to possession, the Devil, who represented libidinal impulses, fantasies and affects which have been split off from the controlling ego to take effect on their own, provided relief of the superego. According to Mentzos, this is the most important function of the formation of symptoms of hysteria. What is more, the conflict which makes libidinal gratification impossible is not an external one but has been internalised through commands and prohibitions. It is not compatible with the superego and the ego-ideal (Mentzos 1980, pp. 23, 57). Psychoanalysts have questioned and reformulated the meaning of the oedipal problems relevant to hysteria (Hoffmann 1979; Mentzos 1980, 1996). 'From a classic psychoanalytic perspective hysteria is linked with genitality, while today's clinical practice underlines the importance of pre-genital fixations' (Green 1976, p. 630).

Mentzos (1996) says the common aspect of the great variety of former hysterical disorders and phenomena is to be seen in the means of overcoming conflicts and not, as was previously the case, in the acceptance of a uniform, oedipal conflict. He hypothesises that oedipal as well as oral and narcissistic conflicts are warded off, pseudo-resolved or compensated for by the people affected, who, in the course of an unconscious process, appear to themselves as well as to others as being different from who they actually are. Both the conversion symptoms and the dissociative disturbances eventually promote the achievement of this goal (Mentzos 1996, p. 92). It is not the intensity of the affect or the apparent lack of an affect that characterises hysteria. Instead hysteria is a reversal into the opposite. When a patient speaks, apparently impassively, about the paralysis of his legs, this hides an opposite affect (p. 97).

The patients' defences veil the situation, serving to negate through the opposite but also compromised satisfaction resulting from acting under false pretences and feigned emphasis, as well as over-activation of the opposite. The hysterical mode is necessary, both because of unbearable feelings of guilt, but also in connection with the also unbearable shame (Mentzos 1996, p. 99). The oedipal conflict is triangular in every case; but in the hysterical mode there can also be dyadic conflicts. The theatrical quality of hysteria reflects the existence of an internal and an external censure. Hysterical patients stand out because they are not ashamed of the affects they display. The mode serves as a defence against shame and guilt. The defence tends to state the opposite of what is true. This involves a false affect that is created for the purpose of putting on a show and a real affect that has been warded off. The affects are not pathological; they are only used in the sense discussed here. The hysterical stagings with their oedipal content do not differ from those of other themes, like separation, helplessness, narcissistic woundings or offences (p. 101).

If we consider hysteria no longer as a neurosis with an oedipal conflict, but instead as a mode for overcoming conflicts, as Mentzos sees it, it is easier to draw a line of development from possession to hysteria. For the possessed, the increasing pressure of an internalised superego led to the creation of symptoms, and to the staging of a reversal into the opposite in order to appease the superego and to relieve the ego. While the possessed did not experience the resisted libidinal wishes and the parts of the superego as parts of the self, but projected them onto witches or images of the Devil, they are in hysteria more closely integrated, but at the same time more repressed; thus, the process of relegating them to the unconscious is more advanced.

Rupprecht-Schampera (1996) also believes that there are enough reasons to trace all degrees of hysteria back to a common basic conflict, and to maintain the clinical, nosological category of a uniform set of symptoms, whereby not only oedipal but also pre-oedipal factors play a role in hysteria.

She assumes that there is a constant interaction between pre-oedipal and oedipal factors. In many cases the separation from the mother failed and the father is not available for triangulation. Thus, the girl uses oedipal triangulation in order to solve the conflict of pre-oedipal separation from her mother. At the same time the relationship between father and daughter is marked by eroticism. Hysteria is based on the relative efficiency of this sexualised attempt to solve the separation conflict.

An encounter with the father – a process in which the generation gap becomes blurred – brings the girl closer to the father. However, the process of coming closer together that originally was intended to heal the girl's self might result in further traumas in which the girl experiences infringements and a strong feeling of guilt in a situation of ardent compulsion. This typically hysterical solution of attracting the father erotically again leads to disappointments. The attempt to shut out the erotic experience from one's consciousness is referred to as repression. Incestuous behaviour and feelings of guilt and shame threaten the self. This often leads to an obsessive idealisation of father-substitutes. Thus, the hysterical girl has created an oedipal scene similar to the oedipal complex, though representing a much more intricate defence mechanism.

By behaving in a seductive manner, the hysterical girl tries to draw the attention of an ideal father to herself, thus attempting to make him dependent on her in order to win him as a triangular object helping her to solve her mother conflicts. According to Rupprecht-Schampera, all forms of hysteria involve an oedipal triangular object, representing a progressive solution. It aims at achieving a separation from the mother by establishing a sexualised relationship with the parent of the opposite sex.

Hysteria is a sexualised, progressive defence attempt which makes use of oedipal fantasies to maintain a defence. The attempt to find solutions by means of hysteria may have occurred entirely without a preceding sexual traumatisation, but sexual traumata can play an important part in connection with a sexualised attempt at defence. It is hardly surprising when sexual traumata are found in a sexualised attempt to find solutions. Seduction and sexual abuse are not the causes of hysteria. They can at most contribute to the development of hysteria in a sexualised, progressive attempt of defence (Rupprecht-Schampera 1996, pp. 68–9).

Closely connected with hysteria is the matter of the seduction theory, the assumption of a sexual trauma during childhood in the etiology of hysteria. Freud (1896) initally rejected this assumption, but never gave it up completely. If we see in hysteria the defence mode of the reversal into the opposite and that of sexualisation, which can but need not be caused by sexual abuse, then the question of the seduction theory is no longer at the focal point of possession and hysteria.

While we were able to observe the defence mechanism of sexualisation in the fantasies of witches and Devils of child witnesses as the result of sexual abuse or other severe trauma, we can see in the possessed a reversal to the opposite and the creation of symptoms. This creation of symptoms was lacking in the child witnesses. Nor did sexualisation always occur as a feature of possession. For Anna Tschudi, the main problem was the conflict with the beloved maid-servant, who seemed to prefer the sister, as her mother did. The sexualisation can be revealed in possession but does not necessarily belong to the development as the reversal into the opposite, namely the superego conflict. Reversal into the opposite and sexualisation in hysteria can be a sign of warding off a traumatic experience, but they can also be used as a temporary solution for the conflict of adolescence.

King (1996) connected adolescent development with the appearance of hysterical symptoms. According to King, the task of becoming an adult is a struggle for integrating genitality. The genitality in hysteria is seen as a task of development which becomes a new task in adolescence. The former way of solving conflicts now has to be combined with genitality. The hysterical solution can be seen as a negative image of the demand for integration during adolescence (King 1996, p. 147). The tensions during adolescence between omnipotence and devaluation, between homosexual and heterosexual identification, the desire for unification and narcissistic isolation and between insatiable longing and asceticism, 'these variations and polarisations can be considered to be reactions of adaption and defence against pressure, which becomes almost unbearable during adolescence' (p. 148).

Caught between desire and prohibition, regression and progression, the staging subject seems to remain aloof from its hysteria, a victim of the event. Hysteria is an intermediate or sometimes even permanent pattern to avoid the adolescent's demands for integration.

If we compare Nicole Obri (see Chapter 5) who, after going to a dance instead of taking care of her little sister, showed symptoms of possession, with Freud's patient Elisabeth von R. (Freud 1895, pp. 135–81), we see in both cases a dominating adolescence conflict.

When treatment began, Elisabeth von R., a 24-year-old single woman, had been suffering from great pain for 18 months. Whenever she walked, this pain radiated from a barely determinable spot in her right thigh. Up to that point, her life had been marked by calamity. After nursing her father, whom she loved deeply, for a long time, she lost him due to a chronic cardiac insufficiency. Then her mother began to suffer from an eye disease, thus needing constant care, and finally her sister, who had married at a young age, died while pregnant with her second child. In addition to her pain, Elisabeth developed a walking disorder. The development of such symptoms comprised several layers, one of which was the conflict between the duties imposed on her by the nursing of her father and the erotic attraction to a secret friend. The patient talked about how she left her father's bedside in order to go out and meet the friend, and how, after coming home late at night, she reproached herself severely for having left her father alone, because his condition had worsened in the meantime. Here, the conversion can be understood as the rejection of an erotic desire.

Another symptomatic layer is also connected with her father. The spot on her thigh from which the pain spread was exactly the spot that touched her father's leg when she swathed him. The current conflict, which was backed with an oedipal subject consisted of the erotic attraction to the boyfriend and the obligation of nursing her father.

While in Nicole Obri's case the emphasis lies on her mother's curse and Nicole's punishment by the Devil, that is, the conflict seems to be dominated by a maternal superego, Elisabeth's case is more strongly marked by the progressive solution through sexualisation and flight to the oedipal object.

Green (1976, p. 645) describes the basic conflict of hysteria as the inability to harmonise the sexual experience with a new object of phallic meaning and the preservation of the parental love object. Studying the saintly women of the thirteenth, fourteenth and fifteenth centuries, we can discern the beginning of an attempted progressive solution (the search for an oedipal object), namely the idea of being the bride of Christ who is repulsed during the struggle with the Devil, as well as the subjection to external forces in order to appease the superego. But the ascetic solution, the avoidance of oedipal conflicts and self-punishment, is still predominant.

In the case of the possessed, the superego pressure is more internalised. They find relief by projecting their feelings of guilt on the accusation of witches, the superego conflict is re-externalised. Reversal into the opposite becomes the dominating mode. Instead of punishing themselves, the possessed women now accuse the Devil or a witch of doing something or other with them, that is, the superego conflict is more and more internalised. Apart from reversal into the opposite, hysterical women increasingly make use of sexualisation and search for an oedipal object to resolve pre-genital conflicts, but also in connection with the repulsion of seduction and sexual abuse. Instead of externalising the conflict by accusing people of being witches or Devils, hysterical women increasingly try to resolve the conflict by sexualising the oedipal object. In the case of child witnesses, witch and Devil fantasies provided an opportunity to ward off a traumatisation through sexualisation and – by means of projective identification – to relieve aggression and feelings of guilt by accusing women of being witches.

Witches and Living Saints Today?

According to Kohut (1975, p. 225), aggression is most dangerous and its destructive powers are most devastating, when they are connected to archaic, omnipotent self- and object-images. The witch persecutions are a terrifying example of this.

In the beginning of the Modern Age, the witch was the image of the refusing mother who punishes individual autonomy and sexuality and who does not suppress her own libidinal drives. This bad-mother imago was projected on to women during the time of the witchcraft accusations. Surprisingly, the notion of witches during the women's movement of the 1970s was the imago of the good mother, the wise medicine woman who disposed of herbal knowledge and who had also integrated sexuality and aggression into the self: 'Tremble, tremble, the witches are back', was the slogan of the 1970s. The witch became the idealised self-image of women, which means that once again a reversal into the opposite had taken place. The witch became the contrasting image of a suppressed woman, who turned round her feelings of aggression and guilt upon herself. The identification with the witch image helped to turn aggression and sexuality toward the outside and thus supported the psychic development of the women in the 1970s. The magically exaggerated contrasting images of culturally desired female suppression introduce important stages of psychic development. During the Early Modern Age, the image of the witch served to dethrone the Mother of God, and to dissolve ascetic avoidances of oedipal conflicts. The fear of witches who exhibited immoral behaviour arose in the transition from the maternal, externalised superego structures to individual, internalised superego structures. Today, identification with the witch allows women to avenge the disadvantages they suffer, and thereby to show aggression rather than depression. The image of the witch has only a psychic function; it has no historical reality. What is dangerous about the image of the witch is its projection on to real women. Must the woman continue to be reduced to motherhood as an ascetic solution or can she also be phallic and oedipal?

Is the reason for the fact that the image of powerful women acting in a phallic manner and at the same time claiming pronounced autonomy and sexuality (in witchcraft imagery, therefore, an oedipal seductress) which so threatens maturing men, is this reason to be found in the phenomenon that to men, the oral and oedipal object is the same and thus the overwhelming object? Yet the answer appears not to be this simple, because, seen within an ethno-psychoanalytic framework, there are numerous cultures in which powerful women are not the subjects of anxiety (Heinemann 1995, 1997, 1998). There, women possess not only imaginary power, but also real power. Is it once again the guilty conscience at work when women are discriminated against and repressed? Is it the guilty conscience that is expressed in the projected anxiety of revenge and that makes women appear so threatening?

" We often hear of the very real frustrations imposed by external reality, but less often hear of the relief and satisfaction it affords. Real milk is satisfying as compared with imaginary milk, but this is not the point. The point is, that in fantasy, things work by magic: there are no brakes on fantasy, and love and hate cause alarming effects. External reality has brakes on it, and can be studied and known, and, in fact, fantasy is only tolerable at full blast when objective reality is appreciated well. The subjective has tremendous value but is so alarming and magical that it cannot be enjoyed except as a parallel to the objective. (Winnicott 1975, p. 153)

There is only one way for women not to become victims of the imaginary power imagines seeking revenge for discrimination: Women have to attain real power, equality, and appreciation in society.

Bibliography

Ahrendt-Schulte, I. (1994) *Weise Frauen – böse Weiber. Die Geschichte der Hexen in der Frühen Neuzeit*, Freiburg.
—— (1995) 'Schadenzauber und Konflikte' in Opitz, C. (ed.), *Der Hexenstreit. Frauen in der frühneuzeitlichen Hexenverfolgung*, Freiburg.
Appel, H. (1937) *Die Wechselbalgsage*, Berlin.
Aries, P.H. (1976) *Studien zur Geschichte des Todes im Abendland*, München.
Arnold, K. (1980) *Kind und Gesellschaft in Mittelalter und Renaissance*, Paderborn.
Attali, J. (1981) *Die kannibalische Ordnung*, Frankfurt am Main.
Badinter, E. (1984) *Die Mutterliebe, Geschichte eines Gefühls vom 17. Jahrhundert bis heute*, München.
—— (1981) *The Myth of Motherhood. A Historical View of the Maternal Instinct*, Flammarion, London.
Baschwitz, K. (1990) *Hexen und Hexenprozesse. Die Geschichte eines Massenwahns und seiner Bekämpfung*, München.
Bastian, T. and Hilgers, M. (1990) 'Kain. Die Trennung von Scham und Schuld am Beispiel der Genesis', *Psyche* 44: 1100–11.
Bayne-Powell, R. (1939) *The English Child in the 18th Century*, London.
Becker, G. et al. (1977) 'Zum kulturellen Bild und zur realen Situation der Frau im Mittelalter und in der frühen Neuzeit' in Becker, G. et al. (eds), *Aus der Zeit der Verzweiflung. Zur Genese und Aktualität des Hexenbildes*, Frankfurt am Main.
Behringer, W. (1987a) 'Vom Unkraut unter dem Weizen, Die Stellung der Kirchen zum Hexenproblem' in Dülmen, R.v. (ed.), *Hexenwelten, Magie und Imagination*, Frankfurt am Main.
—— (1987b) 'Erhob sich das ganze Land zu ihrer Ausrottung ..., Hexenprozesse und Hexenverfolgungen in Europa' in Dülmen, R.v. (ed.), *Hexenwelten, Magie und Imagination*, Frankfurt am Main.
—— (1987c), *Hexenverfolgung in Bayern. Volksmagie, Glaubenseifer und Staatsräson in der Frühen Neuzeit*, München
—— (1988), *Mit dem Feuer vom Leben zum Tod. Hexengesetzgebung in Bayern*, München
Bell, R.M. (1985) *Holy Anorexia*, University of Chicago Press, Chicago and London.

Bigras, J. (1975) *Gute Mutter – Böse Mutter. Das Bild des Kindes von der Mutter*, München
Brackert, H. (1977a) 'Unglückliche, was hast du gehofft? Zu den Hexenbüchern des 15. bis 17. Jahrhunderts' in Becker, G. et al. (eds), *Aus der Zeit der Verzweiflung. Zur Genese und Aktualität des Hexenbildes*, Frankfurt am Main.
—— (1977b) 'Daten und Materialien zur Hexenverfolgung' in Becker, G. et al. (eds), *Aus der Zeit der Verzweiflung. Zur Genese und Aktualität des Hexenbildes*, Frankfurt am Main.
Brenner, I. and Morgenthal, G. (1977) 'Sinnlicher Widerstand während der Ketzer- und Hexenverfolgungen. Materialien und Interpretationen' in Becker, G. et al. (eds), *Aus der Zeit der Verzweiflung. Zur Genese und Aktualität des Hexenbildes*, Frankfurt am Main.
Brumberg, J.J. (1988) *Fasting Girls. The History of Anorexia Nervosa*, Harvard University Press, Cambridge, MA.
Brunner, J. (1996) 'Die Macht der Phantasie – die Phantasie der Macht. Freud und die Politik der Religion', *Psyche* 50: 786–816.
Charcot, J.M. (1886) *Neue Vorlesungen über die Krankheiten des Nervensystems, insbesondere über Hysterie. Autorisierte deutsche Ausgabe von Dr. Sigmund Freud*, Leipzig and Wien.
Chasseguet-Smirgel, J. (1987) *Das Ichideal. Psychoanalytischer Essay über die 'Krankheit der Idealität'*, Frankfurt.
Chodorow, N. (1978) *The Reproduction of Mothering. Psychoanalysis and the Sociology of Gender*, Regents of the University of California.
Cohn, N. (1975) *Europe's Inner Demons. An Enquiry Inspired by the Great Witch-Hunt*, Basic Books, New York.
Collomb, H. (1978) '"Hexerei-Menschenfresserei" und Zweierbeziehung', *Psyche* 32: 463–82.
deMause, L. (1974) 'The Evolution of Childhood' in deMause, L. (ed.), *The History of Childhood*, The Psychohistory Press, New York.
Demos, J. (1982) *Entertaining Satan. Witchcraft and the Culture of Early New England*, Oxford.
Despert, J.L. (1970) *The Emotionally Disturbed Child – Then and Now*, New York.
Devereux, G. (1967) *From Anxiety to Method in the Behavioral Sciences*, Mouton & Co., Paris.
—— (1982) *Normal und anormal. Aufsätze zur allgemeinen Ethnopsychiatrie*, Frankfurt.
Dinzelbacher, P. (1995) *Heilige oder Hexen? Schicksale auffälliger Frauen in Mittelalter und Frühneuzeit*, Zürich.
—— (1996) *Angst im Mittelalter. Teufels-, Todes- und Gotteserfahrung: Mentalitätsgeschichte und Ikonographie*, Paderborn.

Dornes, M. (1993) *Der kompetente Säugling. Die präverbale Entwicklung des Menschen*, Frankfurt am Main.
—— (1997) *Die frühe Kindheit. Entwicklungspsychologie der ersten Lebensjahre*, Frankfurt am Main.
Dülmen, R.v. (1982) *Entstehung des frühneuzeitlichen Europa 1550-1 648*, Fischer Weltgeschichte vol. 24, Frankfurt am Main.
—— (1987) 'Imaginationen des Teuflischen' in Dülmen, R.v. (ed.), *Hexenwelten, Magie und Imagination*, Frankfurt am Main.
—— (1991) *Frauen vor Gericht. Kindsmord in der Frühen Neuzeit*, Frankfurt am Main.
Duerr, H.P. (1979) *Traumzeit*, Frankfurt am Main.
Elias, N. (1976) *Über den Prozeß der Zivilisation, 2 vols*, Frankfurt am Main.
—— (1978) *The Civilizing Process, vol. 1, The History of Manners*, Blackwell, Oxford.
—— (1982) *The Civilizing Process, vol. 2, State Formation and Civilization*, Blackwell, Oxford.
Erikson, E.H. (1975) *Der junge Mann Luther*, Frankfurt am Main.
Ernst, C. (1972) *Teufelsaustreibungen*, Bern.
Frazer, J.G. (1887) *Totemism and Exogamy*, Edinburgh.
—— (1910) *The Golden Bough*, Macmillan, London.
Freud, S. (1895) *Studies on Hysteria* (including Breuer's contribution), in J. Strachey (ed.) *Standard Edition of the Complete Psychological Works of Sigmund Freud*, Hogarth, London, 1953–1973, *S.E. II.*
—— (1896) 'Further Remarks on the Neuro-Psychoses of Defence', *S.E. III*: 159.
—— (1888) 'Aphasie', in Villaret, A., *Handwörterbuch der gesamten Medizin*, vol. 1.
—— (1905) 'Fragment of an Analysis of a Case of Hysteria', *S.E. VII* : 3.
—— (1907) 'Obsessive Actions and Religious Practices', *S.E. IX:* 116.
—— (1908) 'Hysterical Phantasies and their Relation to Bisexuality', *S.E. IX:* 157.
—— (1912) *Totem and Taboo*, *S.E. XIII*: 1.
—— (1913) 'The Disposition to Obsessional Neurosis', *S.E. XII*: 313.
—— (1921) *Group Psychology and the Analysis of the Ego*, *S.E. XVIII:* 69.
—— (1923a) *The Ego and the Id*, *S.E. XIX*: 3.
—— (1923b) 'A Seventeenth Century Demonological Neurosis', *S.E. XIX:* 69.
—— (1924a) 'The Economic Problem of Masochism', *S.E. XIX:* 157.
—— (1924b) 'The Dissolution of the Oedipus Complex', *S.E. XIX:* 173.

—— (1927) *The Future of an Illusion*, S.E. XXI: 3.
—— (1930) *Civilization and its Discontents*, S.E. XXI: 59.
—— (1938) 'Moses and Monotheism', S.E. XXIII: 3.
—— (1956) 'Bericht über meine mit Universitäts-Jubiläums-Reisestipendium unternommene Studienreise nach Paris und Berlin Oktober 1885 – Ende März 1886', *G.W.*, supplement, pp. 31–44.
—— (1985) *The Complete Letters of Sigmund Freud to Wilhelm Fließ 1887–1904*, ed. J.M. Masson, Harvard University Press, London.
Gay, P. (1985) *Freud for Historians*, Oxford University Press, Oxford.
Ginzburg, C. (1990) *Hexensabbat. Entzifferung einer nächtlichen Geschichte*, Berlin.
Goldberg, A. (1975) 'A Fresh Look at Perverse Behaviour', *International Journal of Psycho-Analysis* 56: 335–42.
Graf, A. (1936) *Naturgeschichte des Teufels*, Jena.
Green, A. (1976) 'Die Hysterie' in Eicke, D. (ed.), *Die Psychologie des 20. Jahrhunderts, Vol. 2*, Kindler, Zürich, 623–51.
Greenson, R.R. (1968) 'Dis-identifying from Mother: Its Special Importance for the Boy', *International Journal of Psycho-Analysis*, 49: 370–4.
Grigulevic, J.R. (1976) *Ketzer-Hexen-Inquisitoren (13.–20. Jahrhundert)*, 2 vols, Berlin.
Grunberger, B. (1974) 'Gedanken zum frühen Über-Ich', *Psyche* 29: 508–29.
Habermas, T. (1990) *Heißhunger. Historische Bedingungen der Bulimia nervosa*, Frankfurt am Main.
Haffter, C. (1968) 'The Changeling: History and Psychodynamics of Attitudes to Handicapped Children in European Folklore', *Journal of the History of the Behavioral Sciences* 4: 55ff.
Hammes, M. (1977) *Hexenwahn und Hexenprozesse*, Frankfurt am Main.
Hansen, J. (1963) *Quellen und Untersuchungen zur Geschichte des Hexenwahns und der Hexenverfolgungen im Mittelalter*, Hildesheim.
—— (1964) *Zauberwahn, Inquisition und Hexenprozeß im Mittelalter und die Entstehung der großen Hexenverfolgung*, Aalen.
Hasler, E. (1982) *Anna Göldin, letzte Hexe*, Zürich.
Haustein, J. (1990) *Martin Luther's Stellung zum Zauber- und Hexenwesen, Münchener Kirchenhistorische Studien* vol. 2, Stuttgart.
Heinemann, E. (1995) *Die Frauen von Palau. Zur Ethnoanalyse einer mutterrechtlichen Kultur*, Frankfurt am Main.
—— (1996) *Aggression verstehen und bewältigen*, Heidelberg.
—— (1997) *Das Erbe der Sklaverei. Eine ethnopsychoanalytische*

Studie in Jamaika, Frankfurt am Main. (*The Heritage of Slavery. An Ethnopsychoanalytic Study in Jamaica*, Kingston Publishers, Jamaica, 1999)

—— (1998) 'Fakafefine – Männer, die wie Frauen sind. Inzesttabu und Transsexualität in Tonga (Pazifik)', *Psyche* 52: 472–98.

Heinemann, E. and De Groef, J. (eds) (1999) *Psychoanalysis and Mental Handicap*, Free Association Books, London.

Heinemann, E. et al. (1992) *Gewalttätige Kinder. Psychoanalyse und Pädagogik in Schule, Heim und Therapie*, Frankfurt am Main.

Heinrichs, H.J. (ed.) (1982) *Das Fremde verstehen. Gespräche über Alltag, Normalität und Anormalität*, Frankfurt.

Heinsohn, G. et al. (1979) *Menschenproduktion, Allgemeine Bevölkerungslehre der Neuzeit*, Frankfurt am Main.

Heinsohn, G. and Steiger, O. (1987) *Warum mußte das Speculum zweimal erfunden werden? Kritische Justiz* 2: 200ff.

Hoffmann, S.O. (1979) *Charakter und Neurose*, Suhrkamp, Frankfurt.

Honegger, C. (1977) 'Die Hexen der Neuzeit. Analysen zur anderen Seite der okzidentalen Rationalisierung', in Honegger, C. (ed.), *Die Hexen der Neuzeit. Studien zur Sozialgeschichte eines kulturellen Deutungsmusters*, Frankfurt am Main.

Hunt, D. (1970) *Parents and Children in History*, New York.

Illick, J.E. (1974) 'Child-Rearing in Seventeenth-Century England and America' in DeMause, L. (ed.), *The History of Childhood*, New York.

—— (1982) 'Kindererziehung in England und Amerika im siebzehnten Jahrhundert' in DeMause, L. (ed.), *Hört ihr die Kinder weinen? Eine psychogenetische Geschichte der Kindheit*, Frankfurt am Main.

Irsigler, F. and Lasotta, A. (1989) *Bettler und Gaukler, Dirnen und Henker. Außenseiter in einer mittelalterlichen Stadt Köln 1300 – 1600*, München.

Jacobson, E. (1973) *Das Selbst und die Welt der Objekte*, Frankfurt am Main.

Jones, E. (1912) *Der Alptraum in seiner Beziehung zu gewissen Formen des mittelalterlichen Aberglaubens*, Leipzig.

—— (1972) 'Eine psychoanalytische Studie über den Heiligen Geist' in Spiegel, Y. (ed.), *Psychoanalytische Interpretationen biblischer Texte*, München.

Kellum, B.A. (1974) 'Infanticide in England in the Later Middle Ages', *History of Childhood Quarterly* 1: 367ff.

Kernberg, O.F. (1967) 'Borderline Personality Organization', *Journal of the American Psycho-Analysis Association* 15: 641–85.

—— (1975) *Borderline Conditions and Pathological Narcissism*, Aronson, New York.

—— (1976) *Object Relations Theory and Clinical Psychoanalysis* Aronson, New York.
—— (1978) *Borderline-Störungen und pathologischer Narzißmus*, Frankfurt am Main.
—— (1981) *Objekt-Beziehungen und Praxis der Psychoanalyse*, Stuttgart.
—— (1989) *Objektbeziehungen und Praxis der Psychoanalyse*, Stuttgart.
Kimmerle, G. (1998) 'Hysterie und Hexerei', in Kimmerle, G. (ed.), *Hysterisierungen*, Tübingen.
King, V. (1996) 'Halbierte Schöpfungen. Die Hysterie und die Aneignung des genitalen Innenraums: Urszenenphantasien in der Adoleszenz' in Seidler, G.H. (ed.), *Hysterie heute. Metamorphosen eines Paradiesvogels*, Enke Stuttgart.
Klein, M. (1972) *Das Seelenleben des Kleinkindes und andere Beiträge zur Psychoanalyse*, Reinbek bei Hamburg.
Kohut, H. (1975) *Die Zukunft der Psychoanalyse*, Frankfurt am Main.
Krause, R. (1983) 'Zur Onto- und Phylogenese des Affektsystems und ihrer Beziehungen zu pychischen Störungen', *Psyche* 37: 1016–43.
Kuczynsky, J. (1980) *Geschichte des Alltags des deutschen Volkes, Studien 1, 1600–1650*, Köln.
Kunze, M. (1982) *Die Straße ins Feuer*, München.
—— (1987) *Highroad to the Stake. A tale of Witchcraft*, University of Chicago Press, Chicago and London.
Labovie, E. (1987) 'Hexenspuk und Hexenabwehr', in Dülmen, R.v. (ed.), *Hexenwelten*, Frankfurt am Main.
—— (1991), *Zauberei und Hexenwerk. Ländlicher Hexenglaube in der Frühen Neuzeit*, Frankfurt am Main.
Langer, W.L. (1974) 'Infanticide. A Historical Survey', *History of Childhood Quarterly* 1: 353ff.
Lea, H.C. (1913) *Geschichte der Inquisition im Mittelalter*, 3 vols, Bonn.
—— (1957) *Materials Toward a History of Witchcraft*, 3 vols, New York.
Leber, A. (1983) 'Terror, Teufel und primäre Erfahrung', in Leber, A. (ed.), *Reproduktionen der frühen Erfahrung*, Frankfurt am Main.
Leibbrand, W. and Wettley, A. (1961) *Der Wahnsinn, Geschichte der abendländischen Psychopathologie*, Freiburg.
—— (1967) 'Vorläufige Revision des historischen Hexenbegriffs', in Leibbrand, W. and Wettley, A. *Wahrheit und Verkündung*, vol.1, 819ff., München.
Lichtenberg, J.D. (1983) *Psychoanalysis and Infant Research*, New Jersey.

Lorenzer, A. (1984) *Intimität und soziales Leid. Archäologie der Psychoanalyse*, Frankfurt am Main.
Lowenfeld, H. (1967) 'Über den Niedergang des Teufelsglaubens und seine Folgen für die Massenpsychologie', *Psyche* 21: 513ff.
Mahler, M.S. (1975) 'Die Bedeutung des Loslösungs- und Individuationsprozesses für die Beurteilung von Borderline-Phänomenen', *Psyche* 29: 1078ff.
Marvick, E.W. (1974) 'Nature Versus Nurture: Patterns and Trends in Seventeenth-Century French Child-Rearing' in DeMause, L. (ed.), *The History of Childhood*, New York.
—— (1982) 'Natur und Kultur: Trends und Normen der Kindererziehung in Frankreich im 17 Jahrhundert', in DeMause, L. (ed.), *Hört ihr die Kinder weinen? Eine psychogenetische Geschichte der Kindheit*, Frankfurt am Main.
Mayer, A. (1936) *Erdmutter und Hexe*, München.
McLaughlin, M.M. (1974) 'Survivors and Surrogates: Children and Parents from the Ninth to the Thirteenth Centuries', in DeMause, L. (ed.), *The History of Childhood*, New York.
—— (1982) 'Überlebende und Stellvertreter: Kinder und Eltern zwischen dem neunten und dreizehnten Jahrhundert' in DeMause, L. (ed.), *Hört ihr die Kinder weinen? Eine psychogenetische Geschichte der Kindheit*, Frankfurt am Main.
McNeill, W.H. (1979) *Plagues and Peoples*, New York.
Mentzos, S. (1980) *Hysterie. Zur Psychodynamik unbewußter Inszenierungen*, S. Fischer, Frankfurt.
—— (1996) 'Affektualisierung innerhalb der hysterischen Inszenierung', in Seidler, G.H. (ed.), *Hysterie heute. Metamorphosen eines Paradiesvogels*, Enke, Stuttgart.
Meyer, H. (1983) 'Geistigbehindertenpädagogik', in Solarova, S. (ed.), *Geschichte der Sonderpädagogik*, Stuttgart.
Michelet, J. (1974) *Die Hexe*, München.
Moeller, B. (1977) *Deutschland im Zeitalter der Reformation*, Göttingen.
Murray, M. (1921) *The Witch-Cult in Western Europe: A Study in Anthropology*, London.
—— (1931) *The God of the Witches*, London.
Ogden, T.H. (1988) *Die projektive Identifikation, Forum der Psychoanalyse* 4: 1ff.
Ozment, S. (1983) 'The Family in Reformation Germany: The Bearing and Rearing of Children', *Journal of Family History* 8, No. 2: 159ff.
Paine, L. (1971) *Witches in Faith and Fantasies*, London.
Parin, P. (1973) 'Der Beitrag ethno-psychoanalytischer Untersuchungen zur Aggressionstheorie', *Psyche* 27: 237–48.

—— (1977) 'Das Ich und die Anpassungsmechanismen', *Psyche* 31: 481–515.

Parin, P., Morgenthaler, F. and Parin-Matthèy, G. (1963) *Die Weißen denken zuviel. Psychoanalytische Untersuchungen bei den Dogon in Westafrika*, Frankfurt.

—— (1978) *Fürchte deinen Nächsten wie dich selbst. Psychoanalyse und Gesellschaft am Modell der Agni in Westafrika*, Frankfurt am Main.

Pearson, L.E. (1957) *Elisabethans at Home*, Stanford, CA.

Pfister, O. (1944), *Das Christentum und die Angst. Eine religionspsycholgische, historische und religionshygienische Untersuchung*, Zürich.

—— (1947) *Calvins Eingreifen in die Hexer- und Hexenprozesse von Peney 1545 nach seiner Bedeutung für Geschichte und Gegenwart: ein kritischer Beitrag zur Charakterisierung Calvins und zur gegenwärtigen Calvinrenaissance*, Zürich.

Piaschewski, G. (1935) *Der Wechselbalg*, Breslau.

Piers, M.W. (1976) 'Kindermord – ein historischer Rückblick', *Psyche* 30: No. 5, 418ff.

Pollock, L.A. (1983) *Forgotten Children – Parent–Child Relations from 1500–1900*, Cambridge.

Priskil, P. (1983) 'Mit Feuer das Gelüst legen. Zur Psychoanalyse der Hexenverfolgung', *System ubw* 1: 10ff.

Romano, R. and Tenenti, A. (1967) *Die Grundlegung der modernen Welt, Spätmittelalter, Renaissance, Reformation*, Fischer Weltgeschichte vol. 12, Frankfurt am Main.

Roper, L. (1994) *Oedipus and the Devil. Witchcraft, Sexuality and Religion in Early Modern Europe*, Routledge, London.

Ross, J.B. (1974) 'The Middle-Class Child in Urban Italy, Fourteenth to Early Sixteenth Century', in DeMause, L. (ed.), *The History of Childhood*, New York.

—— (1982) 'Das Bürgerkind in den italienischen Stadtkulturen zwischen dem 14. und dem frühen 16 Jahrhundert', in DeMause, L. (ed.), *Hört ihr die Kinder weinen? Eine psychogenetische Geschichte der Kindheit*, Frankfurt am Main.

Rupprecht-Schampera, U. (1996) '"Hysterie" – eine klassische psychoanalytische Theorie?' in Seidler, G.H. (ed.), *Hysterie heute. Metamorphosen eines Paradiesvogels*, Enke, Stuttgart.

Russell, J.B. (1972) *Witchcraft in the Middle Ages*, Cornell University Press, Ithaca and London.

—— (1977) *The Devil*, New York.

—— (1979) 'Hexerei und Geist des Mittelalters', in Honegger, C. (ed.), *Die Hexen der Neuzeit, Studien zur Sozialgeschichte eines*

kulturellen Deutungsmusters, Frankfurt am Main.
—— (1980) *A History of Witchcraft*, London.
Sander, L.G. et al. (1993) *Hysteria Beyond Freud*, London.
Schild, W. (1980) *Alte Gerichtsbarkeit. Vom Gottesurteil bis zum Beginn der mordernen Rechtssprechung*, München.
Schindler, N. (1992) *Widerspenstige Leute. Studien zur Volkskultur in der frühen Neuzeit*, Frankfurt am Main.
Schivelbusch, W. (1980) *Das Paradies, der Geschmack und die Vernunft*, München and Wien.
Schormann, G. (1981) *Hexenprozesse in Deutschland*, Göttingen.
—— (1991), *Der Krieg gegen die Hexen*, Göttingen.
Schriftenreihe des mittelalterlichen Kriminalmuseums Rothenburg ob der Tauber (1984) *Justiz in alter Zeit*, vol. VI, Rothenburg ob der Tauber.
Schumacher, J. (1937) *Die seelischen Volkskrankheiten im deutschen Mittelalter*, Berlin.
Schwaiger, G. (ed.) (1987) *Teufelsglaube und Hexenprozesse*, München.
Sebald, H. (1996) *Hexenkinder. Das Märchen von der Kindlichen Aufrichtigkeit*, Frankfurt am Main.
Segl, P. (ed.) (1988) *Der Hexenhammer. Entstehung und Umfeld des Malleus maleficarum von 1487*, Bayreuther Historische Kolloquien vol. 2, Köln.
—— (ed.) (1993) *Die Anfänge der Inquisition im Mittelalter*, Köln.
Seidler, G.H. (ed.) (1996) *Hysterie heute. Metamorphosen eines Paradiesvogels*, Stuttgart.
Shahar, S. (1983) *Die Frau im Mittelalter*, Frankfurt am Main.
Shorter, E. (1974) 'Infanticide in the Past', *History of Childhood Quarterly* 1: 178ff.
—— (1975) 'Der Wandel der Mutter-Kind-Beziehungen zu Beginn der Moderne', *Geschichte und Gesellschaft* 1: 256ff.
—— (1977) *Die Geburt der modernen Familie*, Hamburg.
Soldan, W.G. and Heppe, H. (1912) *Geschichte der Hexenprozesse*, 2 vols, Hanau.
Sprenger, J. and Instistoris, H. (1971) *The Malleus Maleficarum*, Dover Publications, New York.
—— (1983) *Der Hexenhammer*, München.
Stern, D. (1990) *Tagebuch eines Babys*, München.
Taylor, G.R. (1958) *The Angel-Makers*, London.
—— (1977) *Kulturgeschichte der Sexualität*, Frankfurt.
Thomas, K. (1973) *Religion and the Decline of Magic*, New York.
—— (1979) 'Die Hexen und ihre soziale Umwelt', in Honegger, C. (ed.), *Die Hexen der Neuzeit, Studien zur Sozialgeschichte eines*

kulturellen Deutungsmusters, Frankfurt am Main.
Trevor-Roper, H.R. (1970) *Religion, Reformation und sozialer Umbruch*, Frankfurt am Main.
—— (1979) 'Der europäische Hexenwahn des 16 und 17 Jahrhunderts', in Honegger, C. (ed.), *Die Hexen der Neuzeit, Studien zur Sozialgeschichte eines kulturellen Deutungsmusters*, Frankfurt am Main.
Tuchman, B.W. (1982) *Der ferne Spiegel. Das dramatische 14. Jahrhundert*, München.
Tucker, M.J. (1974) 'The Child as Beginning and End: Fifteenth and Sixteenth Century English Childhood', in DeMause (ed.), *The History of Childhood*, New York
—— (1982) 'Das Kind als Anfang und Ende: Kindheit in England im 15 und 16 Jahrhundert', in DeMause, L. (ed.), *Hört ihr die Kinder weinen? Eine psychogenetische Geschichte der Kindheit*, Frankfurt am Main.
Vigarello, G. (1988) *Wasser und Seife, Puder und Parfüm. Geschichte der Körperhygiene seit dem Mittelalter*, Frankfurt am Main.
Weber, H. (1991) *Kinderhexenprozesse*, Frankfurt am Main.
—— (1996) *'Von der verführten Kinder Zauberei'. Hexenprozesse gegen Kinder im alten Württemberg*, Sigmaringen
Weinstein, D. and Bell, R.M. (1982) *Saints and Society. The Two Worlds of Western Christendom 1000–1700*, Chicago, IL.
Welldon, E.V. (1988) *Mother, Madonna, Whore*, London.
Winnicott, D.W. (1975) *Through Paediatrics to Psycho-Analysis*, Tavistock, London.
Wolf-Graaf, A. (1983) *Die verborgene Geschichte der Frauenarbeit*, Weinheim-Basel.
Wurmser, L. (1987) 'Widerstreit im Überich und Identitätsspaltung – die Folgen früh-ödipaler Probleme', in Stork, J. (ed.), *Über die Ursprünge des Ödipuskomplexes*, Stuttgart.
—— (1998) *Das Rätsel des Masochismus. Psychoanalytische Untersuchungen von Gewissenszwang und Leidenssucht*, Springer, Berlin, Heidelberg, New York.
Zacharias, G. (1970) *Satanskult und Schwarze Messe*, Wiesbaden.
Zilboorg, G. (1941) *A History of Medical Psychology*, New York.
—— (1962) *Psychoanalysis and Religion*, New York.

Index

abstinence from food 86–7, 88, 89, 124, 130–1
  see also anorexia
accusations 30–42, 113
  preferred victims 113–14
  psychoanalysis of 34–8
  and social situation 17, 38–9
accused
  relationship with victim 31
  relationship with witnesses 30
  women 38–42
adaption mechanisms 120–3
adolescence
  and hysteria 140
  and religion 130–2
adultery 64
  and changelings 81
affect dispositions 94–5
affects 61, 94
  suppression of 116
  see also drives
Africa, witchcraft 127
aggression 64–5, 94
  cannibalistic 128, 136
  projection of 34–5, 75
  suppressed 101
  and women 142
Agni 120
agricultural cult 23
Albigenses 6
alchemy 59
alcohol consumption 62–3
alms, denial of 38
Alpirsbach, Germany 82
Alps 24
Alsace 16
ambivalence 92–3, 95
American Mohave 118
animals, causing illness to 25–6

Anne, St 69
anorexia 129, 130–1
  see also abstinence from food
anxiety 37, 46, 122–3
archaic heritage 102
Ariès, P.H. 51
Arnold, K. 80
astrology 59
Augsburg 88
autonomy 70, 73, 89, 131
Auxonne 76

Bacon, Francis 59
bad mother imago 46–7, 51, 66, 78, 114–15, 142
Baden-Wurttemburg 81–2
Badinter, E. 53
Bamberg 14
Bandia Waly 127
Bartholome, Regina 111–13
Becker, G. 20
beggars 41
Beguines 40
behavioural science 119
Bell, R.M. 129–31
Benandanti 23
Biel, Gertrud 11–12
black mass 44
  see also witches' sabbath
Brackert, H. 15
Brenner, I. 22
brides of Christ 88, 124, 132
Brumberg, J.J. 108
Brunner, J. 103
Bruno, Giordano 59
burning 3–4, 69

cannibalism 127, 128
Canon Episcopi 5–6, 7

Canterbury 86
Capeau, Louise 75–6
capistrum 13
capitalism 58
castration 64, 67
  symbolic 125
  threat of 56
Cathars 5
catholicism 16, 60–1, 125
celibacy 60, 125
changelings 27, 78–81, 134
Charcot, J.M. 103, 104, 106
Chasseguet-Smirgel, J. 124
chastity *vs.* excess 89
child-rearing 116–17, 118
childhood 51–2, 132
children
  body parts used 27
  and civilising process 115
  deformed 78, 79–81, 134
  diet 54
  discipline 53, 55–6
  eating 7, 46
  living conditions 51–6
  oral deprivation 54
  promised to the Devil 27
  punishment 82
  sexual abuse of 81–5, 111–12
  and sexuality 56
  and torture 14
  as witnesses 11–12, 81–5, 111–12, 142
  see also changelings
chocolate 63
Church/Churches
  and daily life 61
  denominations 60–1
  and morality 61
  mysoginism 19
  state 60
  taxes 60
  and witch trials 15–16
circumstantial evidence 9–10
civilising process 115–16
clan conscience 120, 121, 134
cleanliness *see* hygiene
Clemens XIII, Pope 88

Clement IV, Pope 6
clothing 64, 65
coffee and tea 63–4
Cohn, N. 22, 23
collective pathologies 103
collective unconscious 102, 103
Collomb, H. 127
Comenius, John Amos 59
communion, black mass 44
confessional system 61
confessions 8, 9, 13, 22, 29, 41
  and psychoanalystic theory 36, 110–11
  see also denunciations; torture
confiscation 16–17
conscience 136
  and fear of persecution 34
  individual 66, 67, 68
  see also superego
convents, possession 75
conversion symptoms, hysteria 136–7, 141
convulsions 71, 87
Copernicus, Nicolaus 59
Counter-Reformation 60, 66
counter-transference 96, 106, 119, 120
cretinism 78
culture 99
  and inner conflict 118–20, 122
  and psychic development 118

de Demandouls, Madelaine 75–6
defence mechanisms 35, 45–6, 107, 112, 114
  and adaption mechanisms 122
  and ethnic unconscious 118–19
  masochism 132
  see also projective identification; splitting
deMause, L. 51–2, 54, 116–18
Demeter 22
demons 78–9, 134
Demos, J. 128–9
Denmark 18
denunciations 10–11, 33, 38–9, 76
  by children 81–5

Descartes, René 59
devaluation 48
Devereux, G. 118–19, 122
Devil 5, 6, 8, 43–5
  at witches' sabbath 28, 44
  as father substitute 48–9
  and hysteria 141–2
  pact with 6–7, 24, 26, 44, 48, 85, 88
  and possession 71–3, 141
  protection against 45
  as punishing superego 133
  stealing milk 26
  temptation 49
  see also sexual intercourse with Devil
Diana 22
Dianus (Janus) 22
disappointment, coping with 76–7
disidentification 124
dissociation 75, 76–7
  symptoms of hysteria 137
Dogon 120, 121
drives 61–7, 94
  conflict 132
  and culture 107, 108
  see also affects
DSM 137
Duerr, H.P. 20
Dülmen, R.V. 41, 57, 115

eating
  excesses 62
  manners 61
economic crisis 40–1, 57–8
education
  institutional 53
  revolution in 58–60
eggshells 78, 79
ego 66–7, 125
  autonomy 66
  primitive 135
  weakness of boundaries 37
Elias, N. 115–16
Elisabeth von R. 140–1
'empathy', ongoing 35, 37
England 15, 16, 24, 58

epidemics 65
Ernst, C. 71
Esch, Germany 32
Essex 18
ethnic unconscious 118–19, 124
ethno-psychoanalysis 118–120, 135, 143
Eustochio of Padua 87–8
'evil eye' 25
evolution of man 91–2, 95, 101, 105, 115, 118
  see also psychogenetic theory
executions 1–3, 67
  last of 8, 74
  and psychoanalytic theory 36–7
exorcism 71–2, 73
  and therapy 105–6, 109

fakafefines 125–7
fear
  deficient control of 38
  and psychosomatic reactions 34
  of revenge 33–4, 37, 41, 66
  of witches 4, 21, 43–56, 57, 69, 128–9
feasts/banquets 62
feminisation 125
fertility cult 22–4
feudal system 58
fighting 64–5
firearms 65
Flanders 58
food, and sexuality 131
fornication 24
fortune-tellers 5
foster mothers 52, 53
Fracastoro, Girolamo 59
France 16, 24, 75–6
Frazer, James 91–2
Freiburg, Switzerland 18
Freud, Anna 107
Freud, Sigmund 91–106
  Devil 48–51
  evolution of man 91–2, 95, 98, 101, 105, 115
  and history 91, 93, 116
  misrepresented 107

religion 99–100, 103
theory of inheritance 93, 95, 102
torture 105
totemism 92–3, 97–8
unconscious 119
Virgin Mary 124
witchcraft 103–4, 105
Zeitgeist 92, 95
Friuli 23

Galilei, Galileo 59
Gassner, Johann Josef 106
Gauffridy 75–6
Gay, Peter 91, 106–8
genitals, removal of 25, 32
Georg of Darmstadt 12, 18
Germany
  child abuse 81–3
  economic crisis 57
  literacy 58
  witch persecution 7, 11, 15, 16
Gilbert, William 59
Ginzberg, C. 23, 24
global market 58
gluttony 62–3
God
  and conscience 66
  and the Devil 44, 48, 70
  obedience to 68
  and storm-raising 25
Goldberg, A. 112–13
Göldin, Anna 74–5
good and evil 43, 44–5, 94–5
  integration 70
  and psychoanalytic theory 45–51
grain prices 57
Green, A. 141
Gregory IX, Pope 6
group ego 120–1, 122–3
Grunberger, B. 135–6
guilt 35, 67, 85, 97, 115
Gumprecht, 1

Habermas, T. 131
Haitzmann, Christoph 48–51, 124–5, 133
hallucinogenic drugs 20

Hammes, M. 11, 18, 59
handicapped 78, 79–81, 134
handkerchiefs 62
Hansel and Gretel 46
Hansen, J. 24
Harvey, William 59
Haug, Maria 18
Hecate 22
Heinsohn, G. 21
Heppe, H. 9–10, 13–14, 17
herbs 27
heretics
  Beguines 40
  burning of 6
  and fertitlity cults 23
  and witches 7
Hermann the Lame 80
historical change 116–17
history, and psychoanalysis 91–123
hobby-horses 22
Holda 22
homosexuality 44, 64
hot water test ('cauldron snatch') 13
Hunt, D. 54, 55
hydrocephalus 78
hygiene 55, 61–2, 65
hysteria 103–4, 136–42
  defence mechanism 137–40
  diagnosis 137
  and possession 104–5, 106, 136, 138–42
  and sexualisation 139–40, 141, 142
hysterodaemonopathia 106

ICD 10 137
idealisation 48, 70, 73, 76, 93
identification 132, 135
  see also projective identification
idolisation 95
illegitimate children 64
illness/disease 25–6
imagination, power of 24
Immaculate Conception 125
  see also virgin birth
impalement 2
impotence/infertility 25
impoverishment 40–1, 57

incest 44, 92
  fear of 48, 92, 93, 124, 126–7, 128–9
individual development, and cultural processes 91, 100–1, 102, 108
individuation process 45, 128
indulgence system 60
infanticide 54, 114–15
inflation 57–8
Innocent III, Pope 6
Innocent IV, Pope 6
Innocent VIII, Pope 7
Inquisition 6, 9, 23, 60
Institoris, Heinrich 7, 9, 25, 26, 27, 80–1
integration 45–6
interpersonal interaction 36
interpersonal relations 61, 65
intoxication 62–3
introjection 132, 135
Ireland 24
Italy 16, 24, 58
itinerants 41

Jacobson, E. 66, 67
Joan of Arc 15
Jones, E. 125
'jugged hare' 14
Jura Mountains 16, 18

Kava ceremony 128
Kempe, Margery 86
Kepler, Johannes 59
Kernberg, O.F. 35, 37, 94–5, 133–4
Khünin, Lorentz 82–3
killing 65
King, V. 140
Klein, Melanie 34, 45
Knieper, R. 21
knights 65
knives and forks 61
Kohut, H. 142
Kuczynski, J. 11–12
Kunze, M. 3

Labovie, E. 20–1, 30

Laminit, Anna 88
Lauer, Barbell 32–4
Lea, H.C. 24
Leicester 86
Lemgo 15
Lerchheimer, A. 24
literacy 58
living saints 86–90, 124, 129–31, 132–3
  ascetic masochism 131
  and defence mechanisms 88
  frauds 88
  healing powers 86
  and hysteria 108, 141
  and possession 86, 87
  seen as heretics 86–7, 89
  seen as witches 87, 88
  and sufferings 86
  and witchcraft 124
Logrono, Spain 27
Lorenzer, A. 106
Lorraine 16
Loudun 76
Low Countries 24
Luther, Martin 58, 60
  belief in witches 21, 69
  and deformed children 80
  and the Devil 68–9, 70
  and God 66, 68, 70
  and Virgin Mary 69–70
Lutz, Marcel 85

Madonna *see* Virgin Mary
magic
  harmful 24
  protective 78, 132
  psychic function of 93
  and science 59
Mahler, Margaret 45
maleficia 7, 23, 24–5, 30, 37
Malleus maleficarum see Witch Hammer, The
manners 61–2
Mariazell 48
masochism 132
masturbation 56
Mayer, A. 22

memory traces 102
men
  as accusers 19, 30, 113
  projective identification 85
Mentzos, S. 137–8
Merchingen 32
Messina 65
Messmer, Franz Anton 106
Micronesia 47
midwives 20, 21
milk theft 26, 37, 46
  protection against 45
Mora, Sweden 12
Morgenthal, G. 22
Morgenthaler, F. 120–1
mother
  images of 45, 46, 47
  see also bad mother
Mother Earth 22
mother–son relationship 124–8
mothers, unmarried 54
Munich 1–3
Münster 14
Murray, M. 22, 23, 24
mutilation 64
mutual aid 38, 41, 134

Namur 18
Naples 65
narcissism 96, 135
nature, humanisation of 99
needle test 12–13
Netherlands 8, 15
Neuchinger, Christopher 2, 3
neurosis 95
New England 128–9
New World 58
new-born babies 21
Nicole le Roy 71
Norway 18
nose clearing 61–2
Notker the Stutterer 80

obedience 135–6
object-relations theory 94, 96
Obri, Nicole 72–3, 76, 129, 133, 140–1

oedipal conflict 124, 126, 133, 133, 136
  and hysteria 137, 141
oedipal fantasies 105, 106, 110, 111–12, 114
  and fear of witches 125
  self-punishment 124
oedipal mother 47
oedipal phase 56
Oedipus complex 97, 98, 107, 108
  and hysteria 137
  and Reformation 125
  and virgin birth 124
ointment 20, 27
omnipotence 48, 51
ontology and phylogeny 91
oral aggression 51, 54, 56, 133
oral mother 47, 49, 51
ordeals 12–13, 36, 37–8
orgies, ritual 6
original sin 55, 130
orphanages 54
osculum infame (kiss of shame) 6–7, 44
over-indulgence 62
Ozment S. 53, 55

Palau 122–3, 134–5
papacy, schism 60
Pappenheimer family 1–3, 67
paranoid-schizoid position 45
parent–child relations, evolution of 117
parental attitudes 53–4
Parin, P. 120–2, 134
Parin-Matthéy, G. 120–1
permissiveness 64
persecutions
  chronology of 5–8
  and fertility cults 23
  psychoanalysis of 3–4, 100, 103, 108–9, 142
Perugia 86
phylogeny and ontology 91
plague 65
pleasure principle 96
Pollock, L.A. 53

population growth 58
Portugal 16, 24, 57
possessed, oedipal fantasies 106
possession 71–8
  convents 75
  and curses 72–3
  epidemics of 75–6
  and Freud 103–4
  and hysteria 104–5, 106, 136, 138–42
  symptoms 71, 72–3, 74, 75–6
  and witchcraft 71, 74–6, 103–4, 105, 109–10
primary process thinking 37
'primitive' races 92, 96–7, 101
printing press 58
professional groups 65–6
projective identification 34–7, 48, 75, 76, 115
  and the Devil 73, 85, 142
  process of 35–6
  reintrojection 36–7
  saints and witches 89–90
  see also defence mechanisms; splitting
protective magic 78, 132
Protestants 16, 60–1, 125
psychic affects, inheritance of 93, 102
psychic development 118, 124
psychoanalysis
  and culture 115–23
  culture-specific concepts 120, 121–2
  Freud 91–106
  and historians 106–15
  and history 91–123
psychogenetic theory 116–17
  see also evolution of man
psychohistory 116
public holidays 62
pulling 13–14
punishments 41, 64
  public 56, 67

rack 14, 15
reality-testing 66

reason 59, 100
reductionism 107, 108
Reformation 60–1, 66, 125
Regensburg 25, 32
regression 77
regulations 63–4
relics, worship of 43
religion 99–100, 103
  witches' cult 22
  see also Catholics; Church/Churches; Protestants; Virgin Mary
religious wars 16
Renaissance 5
  and childcare 55
repetition compulsion 116
repressed impulses 48
revenge 30–4
  fear of 34, 37, 41, 66
Rhineland 24
rickets 78
Rieti, Colomba von 86–7
robbery 41
Roheim, G. 116
Romano, R. 58
Roper, Lyndal 108–14
Ross, J.B. 77
Rothar, King 5
Rothenburg ob der Tauber 56
Rupprecht-Schampera, U. 138–9
Russell, J.B. 23–4

Saar region 16, 17
Saarland 19, 21, 30
St Baume 75, 76
saints *see* living saints
Salpêtrière school 104
sanitation 55, 62
Savoy 16
Scandinavia 24
Schormann, G. 17
Schurtz, Barbara 82
Schwarzes Kloster (Erfurt) 68
science, revolution in 59–60, 66
Scotland 16
Sebald, H. 81
Sedang Moi, Vietnam 118

seduction by Devil 105, 111–12
  see also sexual intercourse with Devil
self-accusation 111–12, 113
self-castigation 87, 89, 132, 133
self-compulsion 115, 116
self-control 61–2, 65–6
self-destructive behaviour 124, 130
self-reflection 96, 119
self-representation 106
Senegal 127
separation-anxiety 122–3, 138
sexual identity 98
sexual intercourse with Devil 19, 26–7, 29, 44
  children 83, 84, 85
  and deformed offspring 80
  and power 47
  see also children, sexual abuse of
sexual suppression 64
sexualisation, as defence mechanism 112–13
sexuality 61, 64, 85, 89
  and food 131
sleep deprivation 89
social interdependence 115–16
social upheaval 58–61
socialisation 135
Soldan, W.G. 9–10, 13–14, 17
Spain 15, 16, 24
Spanish boots (leg screws) 13, 14
Spee, Freidrich von 8
spices, excessive use of 63
spitting 61–2
splitting 51, 70
  and hysteria 137
  and possession 73, 75, 76–7, 104
  and witchcraft 35, 44–6, 47–8, 114
  see also defence mechanisms; projective identification
Sprenger, Jacob 7, 9, 25, 26, 27, 80–1
Stanton, Margaret 31
Steiger, O. 21
stigma diabolicum see witches' marks

stigmata 88–9
storm-raising 5, 23, 24–5, 37
Sulz 83
superego 73, 98–9
  archaic 47
  collective 101, 134–5
  development of 66, 67, 100
  Devil 133
  externalised 125, 133–5, 142
  internalised 133, 138, 141, 142
  maternal 135, 136, 141, 142
  paternal 136
  and witchcraft accusations 34
  see also conscience
swaddling 54–5
Switzerland 74
syphilis 65

taboo 93–4, 95, 98, 136
tear test 13
technology 59
Tenenti, A. 58
Thomas, K. 30–2, 34, 38, 81
thumbscrews 13
tobacco 63–4
Tonga 125–6, 126–7, 128
torture 1–3, 67
  and confessions 8, 9, 13, 22, 29, 41
  as evidence 9
  illegal 15
  illegal in England 15
  and inquisitional trials 6
  processes 13–14
  in public 65
  testimony under 10, 39
  and therapy 105, 106, 109–11
  see also confessions; denunciations
totemism 92–3, 97–8, 134
trade, expansion of 57, 59
trances 86
transference 106, 119, 120, 126
Trevor-Roper, H.R. 16, 24
Trobriand Islands 108
Tschudi, Anna Maria 74–5, 76, 77–8, 129, 140
Tuchman, B.W. 79
Tucker, M.J. 53

unconscious desire 94
underwear 65
uprisings 58
urbanisation 58, 65

vagrancy 41
Vaud 18
Vaudois 16
Vervins 72
Vesalius, Andreas 59
virgin birth 124
  see also Immaculate Conception
Virgin Mary 43, 44, 48, 50, 125
  as good mother 47, 66–7, 76
  and Luther 69–70
  and oedipal desires 124
visions 89

Wächter, C.G. von 14
Waldenses 6, 8
Walter family 82–3
water test 12, 37
weather magic 24–5
Weber, H. 81–2
weeping, gift of 86, 88
weighing test 12, 38
Weinstein, D. 129–30
wet nurses 52, 53, 54
Weyer, J. 8, 19
Widmar, Elisabeth 83–5
wise women 20, 21–2
Witch Hammer, The (Malleus maleficarum) 7, 8, 9
  deformed children 80–1
  midwives 27
  storm-raising 25
  witnesses 11
  and women 19
witch trials 7, 9, 74
  and evidence 10–13
  and financial profit 16–17
  motivation for 15–17
  psychopathology 71
  and witches' sabbath 27–9
  and women 18–19
  see also accusations; confessions; denunciations; torture

witchcraft
  Africa 127
  belief in 5
  and envy 113–14
  as exceptional crime 9, 15
  as explanation for mishap 31–2
  geographical data 23–4
  and high magic 24
  and possession 71, 74–6, 103–4, 105, 109–10
  witch cult 22
witches
  and the Devil 25
  extermination of 8
  kinship to 27
  notion of 24–9
  persecution of 5–29
  revenge 31–3
  see also fear; women
witches' judges 105, 109
witches' marks 12–13, 26, 28, 44, 89, 104, 105
witches' sabbath 11, 22, 23, 26, 27–9, 75–6
witnesses
  children 11–12, 81–5, 111–12, 142
  integrity of 11
  relationship with accused 30
Wittenburg 43
Wolf-Graaf, A. 57, 58
women 7, 8, 18–20, 47
  accused of witchcraft 38–42
  and aggression 142
  and the Devil 19, 28–9
  executions of 3, 4
  expulsion from guilds 40
  fear of 19–20, 30–1, 33–4
  hostiltiy between 113–14
  identification with witch 142–3
  impoverishment 40–1, 57
  and marriage 39–40, 130
  old 18, 34
  as physicians 20–1
  and possession 77–8
  power of 142–3
  pregnant 14
  psychic development 142

    rights of 39
    status of 19, 38–40, 77–8
    and witches' cult 22
women's movement 142
Wurmser, L. 132
Würzburg 18

York 86

Zacharias, G. 23
Zeitgeist 92, 95
Zurich 14

Index compiled by Sue Carlton